Womning

Jeff and Barbara Galloway

Women's Complete Guide to Running

Meyer & Meyer Sport

British Library Cataloguing in Publication Data
A catalogue record for this book is available from the British Library

Jeff and Barbara Galloway: Women's Complete Guide to Running
Maidenhead: Meyer & Meyer Sport (UK) Ltd., 2007
ISBN 978-1-84126-321-2

© 2007 by Meyer & Meyer Sport (UK) Ltd.
3rd Edition, 2011
Auckland, Beirut, Budapest, Cairo, Cape Town, Dubai, Graz, Indianapolis, Maidenhead,
Melbourne, Olten, Singapore, Tehran, Toronto
Member of the World
Sport Publishers' Association (WSPA)
www.w-s-p-a.org
Printed by: B.O.S.S Druck und Medien GmbH
ISBN 978-1-84126-321-2
E-Mail: verlag@m-m-sports.com
www.m-m-sports.com

CONTENTS

"I Could Never See Myself Sweating"

For many generations and for many reasons, young females have been told not to exercise. Powerful internal instincts put home, husband, children, inlaws....others ahead of self. But each year, hundreds of thousands of women are getting off the couch, and discovering that running provides a uniquely powerful boost to body and mind with a continuing stream of benefits: better health, more energy, a positive attitude, and improved self esteem. Sue's story illustrates how running can allow positive changes to occur.

For years, Sue got mad when she saw a woman running. "She looks awful, sweat and hair flying everywhere. Doesn't she have a family, a job, a home to clean?" The runner seemed to be selfish, possibly irresponsible. Then, Sue's college roommate, Joan, signed up for a local heart disease charity training program in honor of her mother, who had recently passed away as a result of heart disease. About halfway through the training cycle, Sue had lunch to give her friend a donation for the research fund (and catch up on the gossip). When Sue asked the "roomie" how she had time or energy for such a challenge, with 2 kids and a job, Sue was surprised by the passionate answer from the former dorm potato chip champion.

"After the passing of my Mom, I wanted to do something to fight this disease. No, I didn't have time, but the flyer for the training program hit me at the right time." Joan said that the biggest surprise, was how she felt after almost every run: energized with a sense of accomplishment. Sue tasted Joan's drink to make sure it was tea. As she drove home, Sue looked at the runners on the sidewalk in a different light. The following year, Sue crossed the finish line, with her kids and husband cheering wildly.

Those who are taking their first running steps, will certainly face a series of barriers. "I have no ability. I have terrible form, I have no time, I have too many things to do" At the heart of this sense of uncertainty, we believe, is the fear of not being capable of staying with it—the fear of failure. Many of us feel a greater sense of security when we avoid a challenge, rather than risk the sense of guilt from not following through: if you don't start, you won't fail.

But every day we hear from dozens of women who took the minimal risk, and stepped on the treadmill or out the front door. Even with a few minutes of exercise every other day the reports are positive: less stress, a better attitude, and more things done on the exercise days. Yes, by taking some exercise time for yourself, you push back your endurance, reduce stress, and find that you have more energy for family and other responsibilities. This puts you in a better state of mind, with more time for others. Indeed, studies show that exercisers organize their lives better and get more done during the day. The greatest benefit that former sedentary people report, once they get "hooked" on exercise, is that they feel more control over their lives.

You don't need to have any special ability to run, and research says that your current running form is just fine—close to ideal in most cases. In this book you'll read how muscles naturally respond to exercise by improving strength, endurance and tone—at any age. With adequate rest, and liberal walk breaks it's possible to bypass almost all of the aches and pains. You'll learn motivational drills to get started and discover a wide range of rewards from mind and spirit.

Then, you will be approached by others who say things like "I wish I had time to exercise" or "I wish I had your energy" or "I tried to exercise and I'm not designed for it." This is your chance to plant a seed. Tell her that you are sure, with the right method (found in this book), that she can enjoy exercise, and find the time for it. Then offer your help. When you get someone involved in something that changes her life for the better, it enhances your life also.

After over 30 years of helping thousands of women take their first steps, it's clear to us that almost anyone can regularly run without aches and pains. All you need to start is the desire to feel better, and the willingness to spend several periods of 10 to 30 minutes a week gently moving your feet and legs. Every woman who exercises is a winner.

The material below is offered as advice, from one exerciser to another. It is not meant to be medical consultation or scientific fact. For more information in these areas, see a physician or research the medical journals. But above all, laugh and enjoy your journey. It can change your life!

Jeff & Barbara Galloway

2

Women-specific Exercise Issues

By Barbara Galloway

While most of the principles of physiology and training apply to men and women alike, there are some significant gender differences. Men tend to have larger and stronger muscles, more testosterone and stronger bones than women. Women have wider/flexible hips, and greater fat storage. After coaching many women for over 30 years, we've found that women runners have more patience, tend to be more aware of the changes (especially hormonal) in their bodies, place great value in long term health, and are more likely to back off before running aches become injuries. In this chapter we will address the problems that only women face—with some resources.

Movement of internal organs

There is no evidence that running will cause the internal organs to move around and be damaged. Experts believe that our ancient ancestors regularly covered thousands of miles every year—probably more than most Olympic athletes today. Some who study this period of primitive human history believe that women made these constant journeys while pregnant or when carrying young children.

Breast issues

Some women are concerned that running can break down breast tissue. I've seen no evidence for this in any research or noted by any expert in this field. There are support and chafing issues which are managed daily by millions of women exercisers. Larger-breasted women may have a tendency to run or walk with a slight forward lean which can produce lower back and neck muscle fatigue and pain. The postural muscle exercises mentioned in this book can help in managing this problem.

Bras

This piece of exercise equipment is just as important as shoes for comfort and running enjoyment (maybe more) for most women. If the shoes and bra are not selected for your specific needs, you won't be very comfortable and can be miserable when you run. You will gain a great deal of control over your running comfort when you take as much time as necessary to select the model that supports you best, and is comfortable. Be prepared to pay significantly more than you would pay for your everyday bra. Remember that bras usually last a lot longer than shoes.

- There are a growing number of bras designed for specific types of exercise, based upon cup size. Enell, Moving Comfort, Champion, and Nike are just a few of the brands.
- Many of the well constructed "workout bras" are not supportive for runners. The elastic in these products (for twisting and extraneous motion in tennis, Pilates, etc.) allows for significant bouncing and stress when running.

- Comfort: Look first at the fibers next to your body. The micro fibers can move moisture away from your skin. This can greatly reduce chafing (see next section).

A & B Cups: Women who wear these sizes can often find support with an elastic compression bra. There will still be some movement during exercise, and sometimes some skin irritation (particularly on long runs or walks) but this is usually minimal (see the next section on chafing).

C, D & E Cups: Compression bras don't work. Look for bras that have cup sizing, and straps that have minimal or no elastic. Strap placement will differ among individuals—so try on a variety of bras to find the configuration that matches up with your body. If you receive pressure on the shoulders, where the straps press down, padded straps can help. Many large breasted women have reported success with the Enell brand and the Fiona model from Moving Comfort. Champion has a seamless underbra with underwire that has also been successful.

Due to hormone fluctuations, many women find that their breasts are more sensitive at certain times of the month than others. A more supportive bra may provide more comfort when this occurs.

BRA FITTING

- Overall, the bra should fit snugly but not constrict your breathing. You want to be able to breathe naturally as the bra expands horizontally. The lower middle front of the bra should be flat across your skin—snug without pressure.
- Use the middle set of hooks when trying on the bra.
- The cup should not have wrinkles. If this is the case, try a smaller cup size. Sometimes different brands have slightly different size cups.
- If breast tissue comes out of the top of the cup or the side, try a larger size.
- The bra should not force your breasts to move in any direction, or cause them to rub together. A secure fitting cup should limit the motion.

- With the bra on, move your arms as you would do when running. You shouldn't have any aggravation or restriction of the arm motion.
- The width is too wide if the band rides up in the back. You may also lengthen the shoulder straps.
- Under the band, front and back, you should be able to insert one finger.
- Generally, you should be able to put two fingers under each strap.
- Try it on and run in place in front of the mirror to see if there is too much bounce.
- Run for at least a short distance if the store staff will let you. Ensure that you have no irritation places, that breathing is comfortable, and that you can move through the running motion naturally.

Chafing issues

During warm weather, and on longer runs, most women have a few areas where clothing or body parts produce wear on other body parts. By reducing the friction in these areas, you'll reduce the irritation. The most common rubbed areas are between the legs, the lower front center area of the bra and just below and behind the shoulder, where the upper arm swings behind the body. You can significantly reduce both friction and aggravation by using Vaseline and exercise products like "Glide" that tend to last longer.

Many women apply the lubricant to both skin surfaces (and/or the garment) before running, and some carry a ziplock bag with the lubricant. As in most continuous rubbing situations, the sooner you reduce the friction, the less irritation. The "compression tights" (shorts made of lycra), have reduced chafing between the legs dramatically. Sometimes, too much material and/or seaming in the shorts or top will increase chafing. Minimal material is best.

Incontinence

The process of childbirth, aging and the reduction of estrogen often results in a natural weakening of support in the lower pelvis. It is fairly common that the bouncing effect of running will allow a leakage of urine. Women who experience this can do the following:

- Do the kegel exercises: visit www.mayoclinic.com/health/kegel-exercises/WO00119
- Carefully reduce your intake of fluids 1-2 hours before exercise—and/or change liquids
- Wear dark shorts and bring a change of clothing for after a run
- Use an absorbent pad in the shorts
- Ask your doctor about a "bladder tack"

Loss of menstrual periods: amenorrhea

Years ago a leading researcher in female fertility reported that a steady increase in weekly mileage could cause a cessation of periods. Within a few hours he received calls from two of the leading female distance runners in the US. The first was concerned that the cessation would signify permanent loss of fertility, and he assured her that this was not indicated by the research. The second runner wanted to know if a certain amount of daily mileage would reduce fertility for that night (this was also not indicated).

There are many stresses in life that can cause the interruption of the woman's monthly cycle: poor diet, low level of body fat, too much exercise, and an accumulation of life stress. When the overall stress and the stress hormone cortisol reaches a certain level in the individual, the hypothalamus in our brain reduces estrogen production and at some point menstrual periods cease or become irregular. Dr. Nicole Hagedorn, an OB/GYN herself, has noted that regular moderate running can reduce stress in individuals, managing cortisol levels.

But the physical stress of running produces cortisol, and too many miles can be a primary cause of amenorrhea. We believe that too many miles per week kept us from conceiving for several years. It took five competitive marathons in 6 months to produce an injury, and the lack of running and one hormone shot during the recovery allowed for fertility to return. In other words, we owe our first child to an injury.

Amenorrhea

by Nancy Clark

The negative aspects of amenorrhea, as reported by Nancy Clark, are the following:

- loss of calcium from the bones
- an incidence of stress fractures 3 times greater than average (24% of athletes with no or irregular periods experience stress fractures as compared to only 9% of regularly menstruating athletes)
- long-term problems with osteoporosis starting at an early age.
- temporary loss of the ability to conceive a child.

Amenorrhea and anorexia

Although amenorrhea exists among women with no eating disorders, loss of menses is certainly symptomatic of restrictive, anorectic-type eating behaviors. The American Psychiatric Association's definition of anorexia lists "absence of at least three consecutive menstrual cycles" among the criteria. Other criteria include: weight loss 15% below normal for body type, intense fear of gaining weight or becoming fat, and distorted body image (i.e., claiming to feel fat even when emaciated), all of which are concerns common to female athletes. If you feel as though you or someone you know are/is struggling to balance food and exercise, you might want to seek counseling from a trusted physician, dietitian and/or counselor. To find a local sports nutritionist, call 800-366-1655 or visit www.eatright.org and use the American Dietetic Association's referral network.

Note: Be sure to read "Overcoming an Eating Disorder" (#6 in the Hero's chapter)

Suggestions for amenorrhea

- Cut mileage 50% for several months. Swimming could be your exercise substitute. Even world class swimmers have a very low rate of amenorrhea.
- Increase your eating so that you will gain 5 pounds. This will not make you fat and often brings back the regularity of periods.
- Eat adequate protein and calories* Amenorrheic athletes tend to eat less protein and calories than their regularly menstruating counterparts. Even if you are a vegetarian, remember that you still need adequate protein. Eat additional calories from yogurt, fish, beans, tofu and nuts.
- Eat at least 20% of your calories from fat. If you believe you will get fat if you eat fat, think again. Although excess calories from fat are easily fattening, some fat (20-30% of total calories; 40-60+ grams fat/day) is an appropriate part of a healthy sports diet. Nuts, peanut butter, salmon, olive oil are healthful choices.
- If your diet allows, include small portions of red meat 2 to 3 times per week. Surveys suggest runners with amenorrhea tend to eat less red meat and are more likely to follow a vegetarian diet than their regularly menstruating counterparts. Even in the general population, vegetarian women are five times more likely to have menstrual problems than meat eaters. It's unclear why meat seems to have a protective effect upon menses.
- Maintain a calcium-rich diet to help maintain bone density. A safe target is the equivalent of 3 to 4 servings per day of low fat milk, yogurt and other calcium-rich foods. Being athletic, your bones benefit from the protective effect of exercise, but this does not compensate for lack of calcium nor lack of estrogen.
- Stay in touch with your OB-GYN. Many women runners have adjusted hormone supplementation, and returned to regular cycles.

Running through pregnancy

by Barbara Galloway

While I ran through my pregnancies, I will never say that every woman should try this. Most can probably do light exercise for the first half to two-thirds of the term. Find a doctor who wants you to exercise, if possible. When that doctor tells you not to exercise (or cut the amount), you know that you should do so. Your doctor can be your "health coach" in the very best way. Most women who are already running or walking can continue for a while. Don't ever push through pain or any feeling that concerns you.

Stay cool. Exercise during the cool parts of the day. During the summer you can alternate walking or running with a swim or water running (or exercise in the air conditioned indoors).

Crunch time—the final 3 months. During the last two months the baby's demand for oxygen increases significantly. This means that it will be very easy for you to become anaerobic during walks or runs that were easy a month before. If your doctor is still OK with your exercise, slow down and take "sit down breaks" between 3-5 minute segments.

It is very common, during this last trimester, to feel the Braxton-Hicks contactions when walking, and certainly when running. Many doctors will tell you not to exercise when experiencing these. In my case, I was told that occasional contractions were normal and if they became stronger or more frequent, I should stop or switch exercises. I did not experience more serious contractions and continued to exercise until the day before delivery.

Exercising after pregnancy

After childbirth, many women find it difficult to exercise. First, you have to recover from your childbirth experience. Coping with hormonal changes and lactation will produce fatigue also.

When you start exercising after the birth of your child, assume that you are beginning to run for the first time in your life. Even veteran runners would benefit from following the beginning level program in this book, and adjust as needed. Start by walking gently for a few minutes every day. You will learn to treasure this time to yourself, or with a friend or two. The best exercise time of the day for me was right after nursing (or expressing milk). Running is much more comfortable when you're not carrying the extra fluid and weight on your chest.

Dr. Diana Twiggs offers advice after running through several pregnancies.

- Generally safe to continue current program of exercise But this is not a good time to start. Gentle walking is usually OK, but check with your doctor.
- Heart rate limitations have fallen out of vogue.
- Keep your body temperature under control. This usually means less intensity, more hydration, maybe indoor exercise (with air conditioning).
- Check with your doctor concerning your limit of core temperature increase
- Running does NOT increase miscarriage rate.

Running/walking while breastfeeding:

- Avoid dehydration and maintain proper nutrition to maintain milk supply.
- Long run/walk may slightly increase lactic acid for the next feed (not harmful but baby may not like the taste). Can always pump and dump right after a run if the baby doesn't like it.
- Wear properly fitting running bra for comfort.

CHOOSING A RUNNING STROLLER

There are a number of different models. Ask several women who use them for recommendations, and cautions. The better models cost about $350 when new. Some running clubs and running stores will try to match you up with women who are moving out of that phase of their running life, and want to sell their stroller.

- The standard wheel size is @ 20". Smaller wheels produce more bumps and don't handle uneven surface change very well.
- A safety leash is a necessity. Make sure that you have this in place and strapped securely around your arm/hand before you start running. If you run on hilly courses, a hand brake is desirable.
- Be sure that the surface and the size of the sidewalk is wide enough. BE SAFE!

Post-partum depression

Running can help women deal with the psychological challenges of childbirth. Post-partum depression is a serious condition and needs to be treated, often with medication. See a doctor!

PMS and menstrual issues

Let's face it, we women are hormonally challenged. If you are experiencing significant hormonal fluctuations see a doctor who supports exercise.

Should I exercise during my period? Most women can, and many find that their best running occurs when the period is taking place. We're aware of at least one woman who won an Olympic gold medal during her period. Planning ahead means carrying more tampons on your runs, charting a route with strategic bathrooms, wearing dark shorts, etc. Dr. Nicole Hagedorn believes that running may be of great benefit during the week before the period, because it helps women sleep better.

Random aches, pains and cramping, are common during ovulation, before and during menses. Unusual bleeding, severe pain etc. should be mentioned to your doctor.

Your energy level can be controlled by eating more often, combining nutrients, and moving around regularly. If you feel abnormally tired, talk to a dietician. You may be anemic (this is common among women who have heavy periods). You should also have your hormone levels checked. Lack of sleep can be the result of low melatonin and high levels of cortisol. While unlikely, thyroid problems may be a cause.

Some of the medications that women take for PMS and menstrual issues can produce fatigue and sleepiness—and other side-effects. Check with your doctor or pharmacist for details.

Osteoporosis

After age 30, we lose bone mass each year. Weight bearing exercises, such as walking and running, have been shown to strengthen the bones (or at least maintain bone density), when there is adequate calcium in the diet. Some strength exercises, such as the ones noted in this book, can also strengthen connections to the spine, and can help to maintain bone strength in this very important structure. Ask strength experts for other exercises that can help you. Swimming and cycling are two examples of non weight-bearing exercises that will not promote bone density.

Technical explanation: According to Dr. John Bell, weight bearing activities create mechanical bend forces in our bones, altering the alignment of the hydroxyapatite crystals that form bone. This causes an electrical charge of piezo electricity that stimulates the osteocyte to lay down bone.

While a moderate amount of running has been shown to stimulate bone density, running too much (and/or dieting) can put exercisers into a caloric deficit. This stresses your body organism, significantly reducing estrogen production. The result is a loss of menstrual periods and reduction of bone density potential. Reference: „The Female Athlete Triad," Running & FitNews, American Running Association (ARA), June 1999. When you add the stress of pounding due to daily distance and speed training, stress fracture risk increases rapidly according to our experience. You can reduce this risk by running every other day and inserting liberal walk breaks during every run.

Prevention: Exercise can help young women, in effect, put bone density "into storage". About 90% of female bone strength is established by the age of 18, and density peaks between age 25 and 30. Those who exercise strenuously and consume adequate calcium have a higher level of peak bone density. "Think of bone mass as a bank account that needs to be filled with the help of calcium and exercise to ensure strong bones later." Catherine Niewochner, MD.

"Although calcium intake is often cited as the most important factor in healthy bones, our study suggests that exercise is really the predominant lifestyle determinant of bone strength in young women." Professor Tom Lloyd, Pennsylvania State College of Medicine. (References: Journal of Applied Physiology Oct 2004, Journal of Pediatrics June 2004).

After the age of 30, bone density tends to decrease with each passing year. The object is to start with the highest level possible and then hold on to what you have. Weight bearing exercise (60 minutes every other day) and calcium intake (especially milk products and dark green vegetables) are two of the best activities to accomplish this. Most can walk, on the non-running days. The US National Institute of Health recommends that those above the age of 10 years old consume at least 1000mg of calcium a day (@ three 8 oz yogurts). At menopause, the recommendation rises to a minimum daily dose of 1500mg (diet plus supplements). Vitamin D is crucial for calcium absorption: 400IU is recommended for adults. As always, consult with your doctor about any individual issues or medical problems.

Bone loss behaviors

- Smoking: if you smoke, or are around second hand smoke, try to quit and avoid a smoky environment
- Too much alcohol: no more than 2 glasses of wine or 2 beers per day
- Too much caffeine: limit to 3 cups of coffee per day, or equivalent
- Simple carbohydrate consumption: sugar, refined flour, sports drinks instead of milk. Limit simple carb consumption to no more than 20% of total carbohydrate consumption per day.
- Salt: if you need to add to the taste of food, add a little and avoid regular ingestion of salty foods
- Laxative use—try to limit to occasional use if needed.
- Restrictive and prolonged diets: diets don't tend to achieve long term fat loss anyway
- Cortisone drugs—consult with your doctor about drug issues

Menopause and after...

All post-menopausal women should consider supplemental calcium and vitamin D (especially if sun exposure is limited) in order to prevent osteoporosis. There are a continuing series of questions about hormone replacement (estrogen). Read about all of the options and discuss with your doctor. While estrogen promotes calcium absorption and reduction of cardiovascular disease, it may increase risk of breast cancer, blood clots, and endometrial cancer.

Research shows that exercise continues to enhance bone density past the age of 50. Studies of middle aged and post menopausal women have found that at least every other day exercise, adding up to more than 7 miles total a week, resulted in increased bone density in the trunk. Walking and running also produced a density increase in the femoral neck bones.

Bone density tests can usually tell you whether you're at risk for osteoporosis. Dr Richard S. Newman, from the American Medical Athletic Association and ARA website, recommends that those possibly at risk for osteoporosis, should talk to their doctors about a "DEXA scan". This sonogram technology calculates bone density in a 15-minute session, fully clothed on an exam table. There are other tests, including a CT scan test. Osteoporosis is indicated when your bone density reading shows that you are a certain percentage below peak density, based upon age.

Exercise, calcium and vitamin D supplementation and medication can help you hold the bone density you have. There are also some drugs that have been very effective in this area (Fosamax for example). Again, talk to your doctor.

Dr. Ruth Parker recommends the following osteoporosis website links:
http://www.nih.gov/news/WordonHealth/dec2003/osteo.htm
http://www.nlm.nih.gov/medlineplus/news/fullstory_38486.html
http://www.mayoclinic.com/health/exercise/HQ01676
http://www.cdc.gov/powerfulbones/
http://www.mayoclinic.com/health/exercise/SM00059
http://www.niams.nih.gov/ne/highlights/spotlight/2003/exercise.h

ttp://www.niams.nih.gov/bone/hi/fitness_bonehealth.htm
http://consensus.nih.gov/2000/2000Osteoporosis111html.htm
http://womenshealth.gov/pub/steps/Physical%20Activity.htm
http://womenshealth.gov/faq/exercise.htm

Menopause: Most exercising women who are going through menopause tell me that they feel better and have a better attitude on the walking/running days. Exercise helps women sleep better, combatting the insomnia that is common.

The symptoms and intensity of menopause differ greatly. Your greatest asset is a doctor who understands the benefits/effects of exercise and wants you to do it. After you talk through most of the symptoms and make some minor adjustments, you will find what works for you. But whenever you have a possible medical issue, run it by your doctor.

Your energy level can be controlled by eating more often, combining nutrients, and moving around regularly. If you feel abnormally tired, talk to a dietician. Thyroid problems are common as we age, and significant loss of energy can be a symptom. If you've tried to deal with your energy loss through nutrition, etc, without success, ask your doctor about possible thyroid issues. You should have your hormone levels checked. Lack of sleep can be the result of low melotonin and high levels of cortosol.

Hormone supplementation is a very complex issue and should be discussed with your doctor. Because of the reduction of estrogen production, during and after menopause, and sleeplessness due to low melatonin, many women respond well to supplements. OB/GYN Nicole Hagedorn believes that when supplementation is advised, that "bioidentical hormones" work better for most women. These have the same molecular structure as the ones produced by your body. As with all important medical issues, check with your doctor.

Our friend Nancy Clark has the following information concerning the issue of weight gain during menopause.

Women, weight & menopause
by Nancy Clark

"No matter what I do, I can't seem to stop gaining weight..." Frustrated with her expanding waist, this former athlete, like others who are approaching menopause, is frightened about run-away weight gain. She started dieting and exercising harder to counter the flab and, over the din of the exercycle, asked, "Are women *doomed* to gain weight mid-life?" Here are the answers to some questions middle-aged women (and their husbands, children and family members) commonly ask about weight and menopause.

Question: Do women inevitably gain fat with menopause?
No! Women do not always gain weight with menopause. Yes, women commonly get fatter and thicker around the middle as the fat settles in and around the abdominal area. But the changes are due more to lack of exercise and a surplus of calories than to a reduction of hormones. Young athletes with amenorrhea (and reduced hormones) do not get fat...

In a three-year study with more than 3,000 women (initial age 42 to 52 years), the average weight gain was 4.6 pounds. The weight gain occurred in all women, regardless of their menopause status. (Sternfeld, Am J Epidemiol, 2004).

Question: If weight gain is not due to the hormonal shifts of menopause, what does cause it? Here are a few culprits:
* Menopause occurs during a time of life when women may become less active. That is, if your children have grown up and left home, you may find yourself sitting more in front of a TV or computer screen, rather than running up and down stairs, carrying endless loads of laundry.
* A less active lifestyle not only reduces your calorie needs, but also results in a decline in muscle mass. Because muscle drives your metabolic rate, less muscle means a slower metabolism and fewer calories burned. (That is, of course, unless you wisely preserve your muscle by exercising)

- Sleep patterns commonly change in midlife. Add on top of that sleep-disrupting night sweats and a husband who snores, and many women end up feeling exhausted most of the time. Exhaustion and sleep deprivation can easily drain motivation to routinely exercise.
- Sleep deprivation is associated with weight gain. Adults who sleep less than seven hours per night tend to be heavier than their well-slept counterparts. When you are sleep deprived, your appetite grows. That is, the hormone that curbs your appetite (leptin) is reduced and the hormone that increases your appetite (grehlin) become more active. (Taheri, PLoS Med, 2004) Hence, you can have a hard time differentiating between "Am I tired?" or "Am I hungry?" You hear the cookie monster answer "You're hungry and need many cookies...!"
- Menopause coincides with career success, including business meals at nice restaurants, extra wine, plush vacations and cruises. Read that "more calories and less exercise".
- By mid-life, most women are tired of dieting and depriving themselves of tempting foods; they may have been dieting since puberty! The "No, thank you" that prevailed at previous birthday parties now becomes "Yes, please."

TIPS FOR PREVENTING MIDLIFE WEIGHT GAIN AND OPTIMIZING HEALTH

The best way to prevent weight gain is to exercise and maintain an active lifestyle. Research suggests women who exercise do not gain the weight and waist of their non-exercising peers (Sternfeld, Am J Epidem 2004). The exercise program should include both aerobic exercise (to enhance cardiovascular health) and strengthening exercise (to preserve muscle strength and bone density). The book "Strong Women Stay Thin" by Miriam Nelson is a good resource for developing a health-protective exercise program.

- Despite popular belief, taking hormones to counter the symptoms of menopause does not contribute to weight gain. If anything, hormone replacement therapy may help curb mid-life weight gain. (DiCarlo, Menopause, 2004)
- Menopausal women need a strong calcium intake: 1,200 to 1,500 mg calcium/day, or the equivalent of a serving of milk or yogurt at

each meal. If you are tempted to take a supplement instead of consume low fat dairy foods, think again. One supplement does not replace the whole package of health-protective nutrients in low fat milk and yogurt. Also, recent research suggests women who drink 3 or more servings of milk or yogurt per day tend to be leaner than milk-abstainers. Milk can help you lose—not gain—weight.

- If you have gained undesired fat, do not diet. If you have been dieting for 35 to 40 years of your adult life, you should have learned by now that dieting does not work. Rather, you need to learn how to eat healthfully. This means fuel your body with enough breakfast, lunch and afternoon snacks to curb your appetite (and energize your exercise program). Then, eat a lighter dinner. Think "small calorie deficit". That is, consuming 100 fewer calories after dinner (theoretically) translates into losing 10 pounds of fat per year.
- To find peace with food and your body, meet with a registered dietitian (RD) who specializes in sports nutrition. This professional can develop a personalized food plan that fits your needs. To find a local RD, go to www.eatright.org and enter your zip code into the referral network.

Also ask yourself: Am I really overweight? Maybe there is just more of you to love. Your body may not be quite as perfect as it once was at the height of your athletic career, but it can be good enough. I encourage you to focus on being fit and healthy, rather than being thin at any cost. No weight will ever do the enormous job of creating mid-life happiness.

Sports Nutritionist Nancy Clark, MS, RD counsels sports-active people at her private practice in Healthworks Fitness Center (617-383-6100) in Chestnut Hill, MA. Her best-selling Nancy Clark's Sports Nutrition Guidebook, Third Edition offers additional weight-management help, as do her Food Guide for Marathoners: Tips for Everyday Champions and The Cyclist's Food Guide: Fueling for the Distance. All are available via www.nancyclarkrd.com.

Links:

National Diabetes Education Program (NDEP)
Internet: www.ndep.nih.gov
National Diabetes Information Clearinghouse (NDIC)
Internet: www.diabetes.niddk.nih.gov
Weight-control Information Network (WIN)
Internet: win.niddk.nih.gov/notes/index.htm
National Heart, Lung, and Blood Institute (NHLBI) Information
Center
Internet: www.nhlbi.nih.gov
Centers for Disease Control and Prevention (CDC)
Internet:www.cdc.gov/diabetes

#3

Family and Friend Issues

By Barbara Galloway

Support is crucial! Let's face facts, women tend to look for support from family members and other women, when facing a challenge in life. When your close friends and family members are behind you as you get into running, the problems don't seem as difficult. Without support, there will be more stress in scheduling and completing your workouts. Simply telling your friends and family that this is important to you will help in most cases. When you recruit your spouse, child, sister and friends to join you as you run (even if the kids ride their bikes), you'll feel a sense of teamwork. Kids and husbands are aware of the positive changes in you (on your exercise days) and are usually not bashful about telling you: "You're not as grumpy after your run—please do your workout today".

Choosing your exercise companion or group

You'll be more motivated to run if your group (or running companion) is waiting for you. Some women call their friends in other cities during a run, and talk as if they are going along the trail together. The bonding during a run often produces lifelong friendships. Secrets shared on a run usually need to stay there. The first rule should be to run slowly enough to prevent huffing and puffing. It's OK if two running companions are at different ends of the fitness spectrum as long as the faster runner slows down. If your companion is going too fast, you can get injured by trying to stay up. Talk honestly about this. There are many training programs that offer a variety of pace groups. Some are listed on my website: *www.JeffGalloway.com.* Be sure to choose a group that allows you to run without huffing and puffing, and follows about the same run-walk-run ratio as you use.

Helping people in need—including yourself

Linda Gibson articulates well the effectiveness of raising funds for a good cause—which helped her get "hooked" on the fitness lifestyle. "Middle-aged women tend to put everyone else first. This is why I chose to participate in a charity event. This way, I was doing something for others but, in reality, I was really doing it for myself. The fact that I had a trainer and started with the appropriate gear was very important to my success. I would have dropped out had it not been for the support my coach and teammates gave me all the time."

The best example I've seen of a charity event (with training program) is The NATIONAL MARATHON TO FIGHT BREAST CANCER *(www.breastcancermarathon.com)*. All of the race entry fee (100%) benefits breast cancer research at the Mayo Clinic and care for underserved women with breast cancer. There are various fund raising possibilites for men and women, including the chance to earn a trip to the event weekend in Jacksonville Beach, FL for an upbeat weekend with a concert. When you finish a marathon or half-marathon, you experience a series of rewards.

When your significant other doesn't exercise

Honesty is the best policy. Tell your spouse (partner) that your exercise is very important to you, and that you need support. Explain the positive changes you've experienced. Extend the offer to exercise together.

#4

Getting Kids or Adults into Exercise

Mothers who exercise serve as powerful role models to their children. Leading by example, and then encouraging children to enjoy exercise is a gift that keeps on giving. Kids learn that an exercise session can increase energy, improve attitude, increase motivation, release stress, and positively impact schoolwork. Studies (listed in Jeff's book FIT KIDS—SMARTER KIDS) show that kids who get into regular exercise tend to do better academically, and in life. When you help people improve the quality of their lives, you'll not only help them: studies show that this tends to boost your immune system.

- Your motivation to exercise increases when you serve as a role model. You'll also inspire yourself to learn more about fitness. Most adults who teach kids find that they study and learn the principles of training better as they explain them to others.

- Get them a good textbook—and a journal—My books GETTING STARTED, WALKING, & GALLOWAY'S BOOK ON RUNNING 2nd Ed, are great guides.

- Start with a little exercise, and gradually increase. Children will often run a lot harder than they should at first, then get sore and discouraged. Hold them back and they can be successful in every run!

- Make each session enjoyable—especially during the first month If your coachee is huffing and puffing, slow the pace, walk more slowly, and make other adjustments from the beginning of every exercise session. If there is any sign of struggle, then stop for that day. Never push through pain.

Low blood sugar

Before starting, if you suspect that your friend or child is experiencing low blood sugar, have pieces of an energy bar and water, etc. about 30-45 minutes before the start. Have a reward after each session—especially a snack to reload that is composed of 80% carbohydrate and 20% protein. On some special occasions, however, it's OK to have a reward snack that may be a little more decadent than usual.

Find interesting areas where you can run —scenic areas, smooth trails

Convenient routes near school or home, will lead to more exercise sessions a year. But once a week or so, an excursion to an interesting area can be very rewarding. It's great to have variety, and you should give your coachee some choice.

On each exercise session, have a joke, a juicy story or a controversial issue

This will break the ice, inject some humor, and result in a positive bonding experience. With beginners (adults or kids) who are struggling with motivation, the humorous moments provide a series of positive reinforcements.

Don't push too hard, but encourage, and reinforce a good attitude

One of the most difficult decisions in coaching is whether to push or back off—whether to use a pat on the back or a kick on the butt. In general, it is important that the person exercise regularly. When motivation is down, reduce the intensity to reduce discomfort. The ultimate success is realized when the new exerciser wants to do it.

Rewards work!

After a certain number of weeks, or after reaching a certain level of fitness, surprise the coachee with a reward. It doesn't have to be something expensive or exotic. The reward allows the new runner to focus on his or her progress, and feel the satisfaction that comes from steady work.

When your coachee is ready, find a fun event to attend

Races are such positive experiences for new runners. Teachers can set up "success days" when beginners can become athletes. Participation and completion is the goal of these events—not winning. Just having a race date on a calendar will provide the beginner with the identity of an athlete that will increase motivation.

Tell him or her about your mistakes

When you open up to your new exerciser with a personal story, the lessons become more powerful.

Don't over-sell exercise

The benefits are so powerful that almost everyone who stays with it for 6 months will continue. Running with the new athlete on the tough days, and congratulating her for the dedication, are powerful reinforcers. But if your coachee is falling asleep during your one hour speech on the benefits of running you know that you've stepped over the line.

Your greatest reward will be an independent, fit person

Take it as a real compliment that your coachee will need less and less of your guidance. This means that you were an excellent coach, and that he or she can find another person to coach, thereby enriching another life.

KIDS PROGRAMS:

A growing number of fitness programs for children can be licensed or franchised in local areas. Here are some of them:

Girls On The Run This fitness program is designed to help build genuine self esteem based upon accomplishment through running and walking and life lessons. "We measure success with the overall manner in which the girls respect themselves and others....how they feel in their own skin".
www.girlsontherun.org

Marathon Kids® is a ten-year-old non-profit, program conducted through schools for K-5th grade children. Over 100,000 kids participate in various cities around the US.
www.MarathonKids.com

Crim Festival of Races, Flint MI, Youth Fun and Fitness Program involves over 10,000 kids from 38 schools and youth clubs. It is a model grass-roots kids fitness program tied in with an event.

Stretch-n-Grow is a comprehensive fitness program for kids committed to helping educators and parents establish a foundation of exercise, proper nutrition and a healthy lifestyle.
Info@stretchandgrow.com

Kidsrunning.com has several books with great program suggestions: Happy Feet, Healthy Food, Your Child's First Journal of Exercise and Healthy Eating, The Treasure of Health and Happiness.

JUST RUN Monterey County is a FREE program funded by the Big Sur International Marathon and private donations. The goal is to promote fitness and healthy lifestyles in grades 2-8:
www.justrun.org

Websites

Information
www.Kidsrunning.com
www.fitnessforyouth.umich.edu
www.fitnessmba.com
www.kidzworld.com
www.acefitness.org/ofk/youthfitness
www.cdc.gov/verb
www.KidsHealth.org
www.fitnessfinders.net

Games and activities
www.kidsrunning.com
www.pecentral.com
www.runnersworld.com

No More Excuses

All of us have days when we don't feel like exercising. Occasionally, you may need a day off due to sickness, or too much physical activity. But usually this is not the case. Blame your excuses on the left side of your brain. When we are under stress in life (and who isn't) the left brain will have dozens of great reasons why we shouldn't walk or run. They are all perfectly logical and accurate. But we don't have to believe these messages. Once you quickly decide whether there is a medical reason for these blasts, you'll usually conclude that the left brain is just trying to make you lazy.

Thinking ahead and organizing your day will reduce or eliminate most of these excuses. You'll find pockets of time, more energy, quality time with kids, and more enjoyment in the exertion. You'll tend to be more productive in everything you do because you have "your time to yourself."

The following is a list of excuses that most of us hear on a regular basis. With each, there's a strategy for blasting them away. Most of the time, it's as simple as just getting out there. Remember, you can be the captain of your ship. If you take charge over your schedule and your attitude, you will plan ahead. As you learn to ignore the left brain, and put one foot in front of the other, the endorphins start flowing, and the excuses start to melt away. Life is good!

"I don't have time to run"

Most of the recent US Presidents have been regular runners, as well as most of their vice-presidents. Are you busier than the President? You don't have to exercise for 30 minutes straight. You will get the same benefit from your weekday runs by doing them in pockets of time: 5 minutes here, 10 minutes there. Many walkers/runners find that as they get in better shape, they don't need as much sleep which frees up a chunk of time before the day gets started. It all gets down to the question "Are you going to take control over the organization of your day or not?" Spend a few minutes in the morning to arrange your schedule. By making time for exercise, you'll also tend to be more productive and efficient, and will "pay back" the time you spend. Bottom line is that you have the time—seize it and you will have more quality in your life. Your loved ones will appreciate this too, because after a run, you're nicer to them.

TIP: CRAMPED FOR TIME? JUST RUN FOR 5 MINUTES

The main reason that beginners don't make progress is that they don't exercise regularly. Whatever it takes to keep you going every other day—do it. Even if you only have 5-10 minutes, you will maintain most of the adaptations. Besides, if you start to run for 5 minutes, you'll usually stay out for 10 or 15.

"People will talk about me"

Many women deprive themselves of the fat-burning, the vitality enhancement and the attitude boost of walking/running because they are afraid that someone driving by will see them exercising, and judge them in some way. Actually, most people admire and respect those who spend the energy to exercise—whether they look like athletes or not. Besides, it's not a good idea to let the opinions of unknown people stop you from doing something that can enhance your life.

"Exercise makes me tired"

If this happens, you are the one responsible. You have almost complete control over this situation. By starting each run with a good blood sugar level, paced conservatively, with sufficient walk breaks, then you will feel better and more energized than before you started. If you have a bad habit of pushing the pace too much in the beginning, then get control over yourself! As you learn to slow down, you'll go farther and have more energy at the end—and afterwards.

"I don't have the right build (or technique) for running"

Just go to the finish line of the major marathons and you'll see an amazing diversity of body types—including those who weigh more than 300 pounds. Virtually every one of us is genetically designed to run. When we run regularly, our movements become more and more efficient and natural. Even if you don't have smooth form, you can enjoy running with liberal walk breaks, while receiving the benefits.

"I need to spend some time with my kids"

There are a number of exercise strollers that allow parents to walk/run with their kids. The two of us logged thousands of miles with our first child, Brennan, in a single "baby jogger". We got a twin carrier after Westin was born. With the right pacing, you can talk to the kids about anything, and they can't run or crawl away. Sorry, they don't have a model for teenagers. Because we were with the kid(s) in close company, we found that we talked more, and got more feedback than when doing other activities together. By bringing them along with you on a run, you become a great role model: in spite of being busy, you take time to exercise and spend time together.
You can also run around a playground as you watch them play, or run around a track while they play on the infield. Treadmills are increasingly being used by busy moms who can run as the child naps nearby.

"I've got too much work to do"

There will always be work to do. Several surveys have found that exercisers get more work done on days they work out. Running (when paced correctly) can leave you with more energy and a better attitude while you prepare to manage your day. All of this comes with an erasure of stress. Hundreds of morning exercisers have told me that the gentle exertion, early, provides needed time to organize the day, while infusing mental energy. Others say that the after-work "workout" relieved stress, tied up some of the mental loose ends from the office, and allowed for a transition to home life. You will get as much (probably more) work done each day if you run/walk regularly.

"I don't have the energy to run today"

This is one of the easier ones to solve. Most of the exercisers who've consulted us about this excuse had not been eating enough times a day. We don't mean eating more food. In most cases, the quantity of food is reduced. By eating about every 2-3 hours, most feel more energized, more of the time. Even if you aren't eating well during the day, you can overcome low blood sugar by having a "booster" snack about an hour before a run. Caffeine, taken about an hour before exercise, helps (as long as you don't have caffeine sensitivities). The dynamic food duo that we use is an energy bar and a cup of coffee. Just carry some convenient food with you at all times.

I don't have my walking shoes and clothes with me"

Load an old backpack with a pair of running shoes, a top for both winter and summer, shorts and warmup pants, towel, deodorant, and anything else you would need for exercise and clean up. Put the bag next to the front door, or in the trunk of your car, etc. Then, the next time you are waiting to pick up your child from soccer, etc, you can do a quick change in the restroom and make some loops around the field, school, etc.

Read the next chapter! If, after reading the excuse-busters above you are still feeling sorry for yourself, you'll see that there are others who've overcome incredible challenges—often because of the confidence and personal empowerment received from running. As a preview, here is Leigh's story.

Running with cancer

At 30 years old, single-mom Leigh was getting her life back together. She was exercising several hours each week, finishing up her college degree in nursing, and taking care of two young girls. Then, just before Thanksgiving, she was diagnosed with breast cancer and told that she was going to lose both breasts very soon.

"With impending surgery, I felt as though everything was a loss. I felt as if the cancer had already beaten me. I would no longer be able to pick up my toddler and rock her to sleep, workout like I was used to or even carry groceries inside my house."

She came out of her depressed state by burying herself in school, going to the gym, and (after graduation) moving herself and the kids back to the family home in Columbus, GA, from Colorado. After undergoing breast reconstruction surgery she developed a capsulation in one prosthetic and a leak in the other one—leading to a series of surgeries that were more serious than the original one.

Four years and 14 surgeries later, Leigh is back in the gym, and is training for a half-marathon. She is so thankful for being alive, for being able to exercise, that she doesn't mind the series of complicated adjustments she must make every day. I'm sure it won't surprise you that the half-marathon is only a stepping stone for her first marathon.

"I stay as active as my body will let me as long as it will let me— not only for me, but also for my girls. In a society that puts children in front of video games and TVs, my girls run kids races and enjoy as much fitness as possible when they can."

 # 6

Heroes:
Former Non-Exercisers Who Inspire Us

1. *Running with cancer*
   "If I had to choose between my old pre-cancer life as a somewhat depressed, overweight, unmotivated and unfulfilled couch potato and my current life with cancer, it's easy. I'm energetic, happy, motivated and love life each day."

   Lee Kilpack

2. *From zero exercise to 200 marathons/ultras in 12 years—* Cathy is 60 and running strong!

3. **Marathon records after 80**—Sickly most of her life, Mavis began running in her 60s and everything changed for the better.

4. **Kelly runs with one foot**—Think about this when you don't feel like running because things are not "perfect".

5. **Fighting cancer while helping others**—Donna Hicken survives breast cancer twice, and creates THE MARATHON TO FIGHT BREAST CANCER.

6. **Overcoming an eating disorder**—Food was Julie's enemy until she discovered that she felt best when running. Food as fuel became her friend.

7. **Sudden loss of a spouse**—Running is great therapy for Dawn, who now directs a scholarship fund run.

8. **Sudden loss of a child**—After her 18 year old daughter died, Marina was miserable, smoked and gained a lot of weight. Running helped her find a positive slant on the rest of her life.

9. **Running through cancer treatments**—Michelle trained for a marathon during chemo treatments, and ran her marathon a few weeks after a double mastectomy.

10 **Cancer comeback: Boston qualifier.** Sedentary Helene was told by her oncologist to get her affairs in order. Instead, she started training for an unfulfilled dream: running the Boston Marathon. With each marathon, she became less sick—and then qualified for her goal race.

11. **Running with lupus.** "People often ask me how I can run with arthritis; I just smile and say 'how can I not'." Rachel's inspiring challenge.

12. **Jeff's hero**—Kitty's story

1. Running with cancer

In 1996 Lee Kilpack was diagnosed with breast cancer, with lymph node involvement. She began a treatment plan of surgery, chemo, and radiation. Lee had never exercised. The diagnosis was a shock to her spirit, and the treatment tested body, mind and will power.

By 2000, things weren't looking very good, and she felt bad most of the time. Then, one morning, she woke up with the desire to start taking care of her body. She hired a personal trainer that day. By 2001, she was walking every day. Later that year she had inserted some running into the walks. In 2002, Lee walked the 3Day/60 Mile Breast Cancer Walk and raised $3000 for the cause.

The training for and the completion of such a strenuous event produced a big letdown in motivation, with extended recovery from injuries, aches and pains. Lee struggled, and finally started running regularly in December of 2003. After the '04 New Year, Lee set a bigger goal: to finish a marathon in November. The training program she chose was too aggressive and she became injured in September. She didn't give up.

In early 2005, her doctor cleared her to start running again. She picked the Galloway (more conservative) training program this time around. As Lee checked in via email, it was obvious that she often found it hard to hold back her energy and drive. The training for the Marine Corps Marathon was more of a challenge than for most because she relocated to the Gulf Coast as a relief volunteer after Hurricane Katrina—squeezing in long runs after exhausting days. Somehow, she also hikes, cycles, and paddles hard in her kayak, on the "off days" when she doesn't run.

Lee regularly gets screened for tumor markers. While the tests show her out of the normal range, her doctor does not see a threat in the near future, and supports her running. "I don't know what the future holds for me. If it is metastasis tomorrow,

I would be OK with that. What a good life I've been given. My health and happiness have never been better. What my oncologist doesn't understand is what a dynamite combo vitality and endorphins make."

Lee is training for 3 half-marathons and 3 marathons in the next year. "I am so thankful for my cancer. My life has been changed for the better and I can't express how great I feel now...I love my body, my running—life itself."

2. Exercise renaissance in her 50s

Over a decade ago, Cathy Troisi patiently listened through most of the sessions of a Galloway running school in Boston. Her energy level and attentiveness picked up when we got into the run-walk-run segment. Cathy had never run before, wanted to do the Boston Marathon to raise funds for a charity, and thought she had waited too long to start running. Even veteran runners told her that running past the age of 50 would hurt her joints. Walk breaks gave her hope. She called me 6 months later, gushing with the excitement of finishing her first marathon. The excitement has not gone away.

Lifestyle before running: no physical activity, ever (except gym class in high school)
First marathon: 6 hours, using a ratio of run a minute/walk a minute
12 years later: over 200 marathons and ultras...and counting.
# of injuries in 12 years: 0
$ raised for charity in 12 years: over $70,000

What running has done for her
• Appreciation of health potential, human performance potential, and to not take health for granted
• More conscious of diet
• "I've never felt my age (now, over 60)"
• Social camaraderie across 50 states

- Enriching travel experiences—shared
- Positive mental outlook and attitude, especially when challenged
- Wonderful new friends
- A chance to volunteer—give back

"Running is a panacea for a healthy life: physically, mentally, emotionally. Aging can be a healthier process due to this simple activity. It requires minimal equipment, allows time for reflection, provides an opportunity to get in touch with nature, incurs minimal cost, and breaks down age barriers." *C Troisi*

3. Marathon records after 80

Mavis Lindgren was a sickly child, and a sickly adult—and was advised against exercising. She almost died of a lung infection in her late 50s. During the recovery, her new young doctor had the shocking opinion that she should walk with her husband, and during each check up, kept recommending an increase in the distance she covered with him.

Surprisingly, Mavis found enjoyment as she felt her body come alive with improved endurance. In her 60s, she took up running with husband Carl, and quickly surpassed him. Into her late 80s she was setting age group records—and had not even suffered a common cold since beginning her running career.

At about the age of 85 she slipped on a cup at the 20-mile water station of the Portland (OR) Marathon. Officials helped her up and tried to take her to a medical tent. She quietly brushed them off, saying that it was a surface injury. After she finished she went to the medical tent to find that she had been running with a broken arm.

We miss Mavis, but her pleasant, positive, quiet and tough spirit lives on.

4. Running with only one foot

When you start feeling sorry for yourself because your feet hurt or your legs don't have the bounce of past years, think of Kelly Luckett. Kelly lost her leg at age 2, and disconnected with the thought of regular exercise or sports. As a sedentary spouse, she watched her husband become a runner, and for years cheered him to the finish of Atlanta's Peachtree Road Race. Kelly had used a prosthesis for years, but thought that regular exercise was out of her range of possibilities.

In 2003, she decided to enter the Peachtree race herself and started walking. She overcame many unique problems relating to the mechanics of the device, and made adjustments. Since the Peachtree is listed as a running race, Kelly tried to run, but could only last for 30 seconds. She gave up many times—re-starting each time.

Slowly, she made progress, adjusting the equipment, the urethane liner, and foot gear. She made it through her first Peachtree, along with 55,000 others, and couldn't imagine running much farther than 6 miles until she attended one of the Galloway one-day running schools and learned about the run-walk-run method. We stayed in touch for the next year, fine-tuning her training and her run-walk-run ratio. We have not seen an athlete with a stronger spirit.

Her first half-marathon was tough and she told us that she couldn't imagine going twice that distance at any speed. Over the next 6 months we kept adjusting the run-walk-run ratio, and Kelly finished the Country Music Marathon in 6 hours and 46 minutes. She passed a number of runners in the last 10 miles and qualified for the world's most famous race: The Boston Marathon.

Kelly was only the third female amputee to finish this premier race. Her training paid off and she improved her time by almost 20 minutes! She's well on her way to the next challenge: a 50 miler.

5. Fighting breast cancer while helping others

Donna Hicken, started running in January of 1995 in hopes of burning off "baby fat" following the birth of her son, Drew. The busy on-air TV news anchor had not been an exerciser before, but "completely fell in love with it." Progressing through the distances of local road races, she finished the Gate River Run a year later, and thought afterward that this 9.3 mile distance would be the longest she would ever want to run.

But in 1998 she got hooked on the marathon journey, and the satisfaction of raising money for a charity. She finished the Walt Disney World Marathon, but now admits that she was overtrained. She continued to try to push through nagging injuries until she heard the doctor say the two ugly words "stress fracture."

While still recovering from a stress fracture, Donna ran the '99 Boston Marathon on the Dana Farber Marathon Challenge team, raising funds for breast cancer research. "Ironically, 7 months after that race, I became the cause. It was only the beginning of a very different kind of race for me."

In November of 1999 she was diagnosed with breast cancer. She struggled through major surgery, chemo and radiation. In 2002, when it was hoped that life would start to normalize, there was more bad news, the cancer had returned. During the second round of surgery, chemo and radiation, there were many dark days when she said to herself "I just don't think I can do this anymore." But she drew upon her experience as a runner.

"By that time I was well acquainted with 'the wall'. You know that feeling somewhere around mile 20 in the marathon where you just want to sit in the road and cry. I knew that I could hit that wall, and that if I just kept going, I could get to the other side. It gave me a level of confidence I wouldn't have had otherwise. I knew I'd be back and I knew I'd be running."

In 2003 she ran the Chicago Marathon as a celebration of being cancer free. That same year she founded the Donna Hicken Foundation. DHF pays for the critical needs of breast cancer patients while they are going through treatment. "Women shouldn't have to worry about how to pay rent and child care when they are undergoing chemo."

In 2005 Donna and Jeff met and decided to team up to train runners for the Jacksonville Marathon. This program (26.2 With Donna) enabled many beginning exercisers to finish a marathon 6 months later—even some who were being treated for breast cancer. Donna ran two marathons that year and believes that it was the Galloway program that kept her, and others, injury free—while meeting new "friends for life."

"The most exciting news is that Jeff and I have decided to start our own marathon! It's the only marathon in the country dedicated to wiping out breast cancer in our lifetime and caring for women living with the disease right now. *26.2 with Donna: The National Marathon to Fight Breast Cancer* kicks off February 17th of 2008 in Jacksonville Beach!"

For more information visit *www.breastcancermarathon.com*

6. Overcoming an eating disorder

Julie was an overweight child, rode horses, ate pop tarts and tater tots, had a wonderful Mom, but experienced self-esteem issues. As a 9th grader (180 pounds, 5' 10") she broke her foot falling off a horse, hobbled around and got depressed, and reduced her quantity of food. As she lost weight, she received positive feedback from peers for the first time in her life ("You look good"), and started to feel good about herself. So she ate even less and lost more—down to 110 lbs!

"I don't remember when, or how, but I noticed things starting to change. I was still getting attention, but it was from those with concern. I started riding again and my trainer approached me and asked me to feel free to come to her if I had a problem because she had been there before. I started feeling light-headed all the time, I would try to stand up and literally fall right back down. I quit getting my period and it was a struggle to walk, let alone ride. Bottom line was that I felt weak, and I knew I needed to do something about it."

She started running, and walking (alternating mailboxes) but was so hungry and weak that she ate more, became energetic and felt strong, settling into a healthy weight of 145 lbs. Then came college. Caring for horses, studying hard, commuting to school took time and she stopped running. "My mind went into a hard downward spiral of self-esteem once again, and I started something new, turning to food for comfort. I didn't do drugs or smoke, but I turned to food for that quick endorphin boost. I would find myself tired, frustrated, and disgusted, and would lock myself in my room literally gorging on whatever was in sight." The scales exceeded the 200 mark, she hated herself, and hid from friends.

"I wrote in a diary every night about how I would change, only to fail the following day. Again, I had hit a very low point and knew I needed to do something. Knowing I could not control my eating habits, I started trying to control something I knew I could, my exercise. I started running again. And again, experienced the same psychological response as I did in high school. I felt better about myself, I started to lose weight, and I was able to pull myself out of the slump."

Julie was inspired: to read about proper nutrition, to eat more meals each day, and to train for a marathon. "My mood sailed and I could conquer the world, or could I? I trained (running straight out) to the point of completing my first half-marathon, which sent me to straight burn out. My runs became a constant struggle, and I started to hate every second of them. I stopped running, and up went the weight, down went the self-esteem and mood."

Julie fell in love, with Chris, and they decided to train for a marathon. "I stumbled across the most wonderful concept, something that up until now my body had known but I did not, *eating gave you fuel.*"

She started running stronger and faster and broke all of her personal records.

"I no longer run because I eat too much, I eat so that I can run. I have dropped weight, but my body composition has completely changed. My body fat is the lowest it has ever been, and guess what, I'm eating Reese's Peanut Butter Cups and white breads! Who would have thought!" *Julie S.*

7. Sudden loss of a spouse

"Running did not take the pain away. After my body adjusted to running it became a soothing form of dealing with the pain."

Dawn Cash started running with a few other military wives in 2004, when their husbands left for Iraq. Perhaps the training for the Army 10-miler could help burn the 20 pounds she gained from worrying. "If my husband could live under those conditions in Iraq for a year or more then I could certainly run 10 miles for him."

"I had been training for three months when I was told the words that no military wife ever wants to hear. The only words I remember hearing are 'We regret to inform you…' that was it. My mind shut down at that very moment. All I remember thinking was that he was ok. After all, we had spoken on the phone just the night before. There literally are no words that could possibly describe the pain that filled my heart and my life for months… even years…. to come."

"Several weeks after Chris' death I wanted to run so I did. I had a couple of Chris' running buddies help me but most importantly I could hear Chris' words of encouragement. In every conversation

Chris would ask how my training was coming along and would always give me advice and 'keep up the hard work'. As weird as it may sound I felt connected to Chris through running. Chris was an avid runner and had run since his high school days."

"I would always think of Chris and what he gave up for my freedom (our freedom) and I always found the strength to keep going. 'One step at a time' which was how I was living my life.... one day at a time. I ran the Army 10-miler on Oct 24, 2004, just four long but yet short months after Chris' death. It was a sad yet happy day. Chris had passed his love for running on to me."

"For a long time I think I ran to get me through the pain, a way of grief counseling (I talked a whole lot during my runs), but I also ran for Chris. I have seen running shirts that say "Running is better than Prozac" or "Running is my therapy" and that is so true. I wonder how many runners run because of problems in their lives."

When North Carolina Wesleyan College established a scholarship in Chris' name, Dawn volunteered to help in fund raising. A running event was a perfect choice. Dawn is not only getting into better and better shape with her training, she is helping others improve their lives while giving meaning to her husband's life. If you're in North Carolina the first weekend in December, think about running the Reindeer for Cash.

8. Sudden loss of a child

Marina, who smoked, started exercising in January of 1994, weighing 200 pounds. With the help of a personal trainer she lifted weights, started running, lost weight, while she continued to smoke. In 1996 she started training for the Los Angeles Marathon, stopped smoking, and crossed the finish line weighing 137 pounds.

In 2000, her 18-year-old daughter, Rachel, died in a car accident. Marina quit exercising, started smoking again, and gained back to

200 pounds. "It took me a year and half to realize that no amount of grief would bring me my daughter back. But every Sunday she would look out the window and wish that she was running the trails on "Mt. Tam".

Marina joined a woman's running club, entered some races, trained for half-marathons, and quit smoking "only because of running—I had to choose, and running won over smoking".

"It took me many years to say this, but I have become an athlete. If you would have asked me to do something new or difficult before, I would have said 'I can't'. Today, my answer would be 'No problem'. Last December, to take her mind off getting older, Marina ran a race with a few of her running friends. She ran the fastest mile of her life. "It didn't matter that I was older that day. I was faster". *Marina G*

9. Marathon training during cancer treatments

"I don't feel the nausea of chemo, the pain from surgeries, the fatigue from lack of sleep—I feel the exhilaration of moving."

Michelle Juehring was diagnosed with breast cancer in February, 2006. Having run every one of her hometown Quad Cities Marathons, she used the September 2006 event as her way of focusing on something beyond her treatment "marathon". This was no surprise to her training partner Jen, because Michelle had finished the '02 event while pregnant, and ran the '03 marathon only 3 months after giving birth, by Cesarean to her second child (including a 7-minute milk-pumping break along the course).

Michelle's first surgery, a lumpectomy and lymph node dissection, occurred one month before marathon training began. Six months of chemo soon followed. Then, only about 6 weeks before the marathon, she had a bilateral mastectomy followed by immediate reconstructive surgery. With all of this going on, Michelle continued to do long runs, as she could, using variations of walk breaks.

Jen secretly thought that Michelle's goal of a sub-6-hour marathon was was "a little unrealistic". The strategy of running 2 minutes each mile was working until the traditional "wall" surrounded them. When the going got tough, Michelle felt the strength of support from her friends: "Because they could be going much, much faster, it would not be fair to them for me to slow down or even quit. If I got too sentimental I'd get sad and then I WOULD slow down." With great determination and a brisk walk pace, Michelle recorded a chip time of 5:55:45!

Jen's report says it all: "Now Michelle is settling back into a work schedule, she has started radiation therapy and is enjoying life with her husband Dave, her son Dane (3) and her daughter Shelby (15 months). Throughout the process she has had amazing family support and she and her husband always use the words "we" and "our" when talking about "their" diagnosis and treatment. Breast cancer impacts the entire family and they are facing it head on while still considering it a bump in the road. Michelle is a true hero."

10. Cancer comeback: Boston qualifier

It started with earaches in 1991. Helene was told that she brought this on by using a Q-tip. But when her coordination deteriorated, she lost her hearing and some awful stuff dripped out of her ear, her doctors tested further. They found cancer in the form of Hodgkin's disease. Helene found herself dizzy all the time, started losing her memory, and lived with an awful headache.

In 1994 she had two operations but the pain would not go away. She went on morphine, couldn't do anything but sleep, and needed help to open her own pill bottle. Another operation at the Mayo Clinic, in 1995 removed a mass from her head. She felt good after that surgery, but was hooked to an IV for an extended period. Most of 1998 was spent in the hospital with constant diarrhea, headache and other problems. In July her oncologist said that her immune system was shot—that she would not get better, and was told to "get her affairs in order". For some strange reason, sedentary Helene decided to train for a marathon.

Searching the web for "marathons" she found one in Chicago in October, and just knew she could do it. So while the doctors were preparing her for finishing her journey, Helene took her first running steps on a dirt road out of town. As she ran, her boys (11 and 13) drove her vehicle alongside and cheered: 600 yards the first day, a little further the second day. "Altogether I ran 6 times. One of those times being 6 miles. I was ready!"

"I bought the prettiest running outfit, and some bright running shoes, the color of the stuff that dripped out of my ear in 1991 and drove to Chicago with some friends. Feeling "pretty cool" in her outfit, she ran until she saw the Samuel Adams beer tent, where there was an ambulance that had been reserved for her by a friend. "What the heck do they know??? I crossed the line 4:28! And went to the beer tent. Ok, so I couldn't walk for a week. But I did it."

In 1999 she trained for the San Diego Rock and Roll Marathon, and finished the 2000 Houston Marathon in 4:00. "I wanted to put myself in pain from a good source rather than focus on the constant pain out of my head." In 2001 she ran in the London Marathon for a charity and qualified for Boston with a 3:40.

In 2006, after more surgery and hospital treatments, Helene is still focused on living life to the fullest. She is working on finishing marathons in each of the 50 states, "and perhaps a few other ideas I have cooking up in my head."

11. Running with lupus

"People often ask me how I can run with arthritis; I just smile and say 'how can I not'."

Rachel had been treated for arthritis since she was about 12 years old, a genetic condition. She was discouraged from exercising, being told that it would harm the joints. Research has generally shown the opposite to be true (with individual differences). In the 1980's, a friend suggested that exercise could be good for her condition and she gave it a try, running about a mile away from her house, and then back. She decided to attempt a marathon and came to our Tahoe retreat for reinforcement.

"I learned that it was not just about running but about eating right, getting enough rest, and 'listening to your body during each run.' And I did run my first marathon in Portland in September of 1989. I was a runner! Then one day in the late fall of 1991 I got up early, drove to Greenlake (a Seattle running loop) for my run, got out of the car and absolutely could not run. It was like hitting the wall only I had not done anything beforehand to cause it."

A few years later, Rachel's doctors began calling her condition "lupus", but it took about two years for her to understand the extent of her condition. "I did not know how much I learned from running and running itself would in the end help me manage my lupus…All I can say is that I was so sick! However, on the days that I should have been running I would put on my running clothes and visualize the day that I would be back out there. With the discipline I learned, listening to my body each day and with the help of a great doctor, I slowly came back. I was determined to run again. It was very hard having built up to long distances to have to start again literally one block at a time. But that's what I did — just built up my long runs one block, two blocks, etc. By 1992, I did one 5K and by 1994 I was back running races, including half-marathons."

"Then I saw the running vacation to Greece to run the original marathon and knew I had to do it. It was one of the greatest adventures of my life. I have completed around 12 or so marathons…I live what I learned at that first running camp – balance. And balance is the biggest part of my management of my lupus. Running makes me stronger and even though I still have flares, I am stronger, mentally and physically, and know I can come back."

Rachel notes that there are multiple degrees, symptoms, treatments for lupus. For more information, visit *http://www.lupus.org/*

12. Jeff's hero—Kitty's story

At the age of 81 years old Kitty decided to enter the Peachtree (10K) road race. One year before, she had finished with no major problems, but things had changed. While she had never smoked, a tumor was discovered in the sensitive bronchial passages near the heart. It was an inoperable condition.

While her doctor was OK with her decision, I asked her several times whether she should challenge herself on a hilly 6-mile course, in hot Atlanta, GA, on July 4th. She didn't argue with me, but in her quiet way, I could tell that my questions only magnified her determination to do it. One of the primary reasons, however, may be the result of having grown up during the Great Depression: she couldn't get a refund on the entry fee, and was determined to get her money's worth.

I believe that Kitty would have had no major problems if the temperature had remained as it was at the start: 60°F. Unfortunately she was in the last starting group which started much later, and the temperature increased every few minutes. She knew she was in trouble at 3 miles (over 80°F with high humidity) but struggled up Cardiac Hill past the 4-mile mark when there seemed to be nothing left in the tank.

A few minutes later, the City of Atlanta street sweeper approached. Most Peachtree participants know and fear the "grim sweeper" because when it catches you, your race is over. Kitty didn't care because she had been physically spent for 30 minutes.

This time, the sweeper stopped. Kitty motioned for the driver to move on. He stuck his head out the window and told her that she was just as important as any other runner in the race, and that he was going to stay behind her until she finished. That's all she needed. It was a real struggle but you wouldn't have known it as she somehow found a spring in her step, crossing the 6.2 mile mark with her head held high.

Kitty Galloway taught me, by example, the principles that are the foundation of my life: never give up, take control over each day, confront every challenge and do your best. She crossed her final finish line about 18 months after her last Peachtree—mentally sharp, with her head held high. She was my Mom and is my hero.

Jeff

 # 7

What Does the Research Say?

Edited by Jeff

"For every hour you exercise, you can receive two hours added to your lifespan."

The evidence is growing that running and walking will bring quality to your life, while also increasing the quantity. According to the research, running (even over many years) will not harm your joints—when done correctly. But every year I hear statements from uninformed doctors who are prejudiced against running, don't read the research, and who mistakenly maintain that humans were not designed for running. This chapter is your guide to the research, so that you can decide.

It's my opinion, and that of many medical experts, that most people will maintain their cardiovascular system better and suffer less joint damage by regularly and gently, running and walking. During a clinic on his research findings(listed below), leading researcher Dr. Paffenbarger stated that for every hour you exercise, you can expect to have your life extended by 2 hours. That's a great return on investment!

Of course it is possible for veteran runners, past a certain age, to cause orthopedic problems by ignoring the rules of training and doing too much speedwork and total mileage, while neglecting strategic rest and walk breaks. Because there are many individual differences, especially during the aging process, you should find the medical experts in the areas that are important to you, and stay in touch about any problems that come up. You'll find suggestions in this book about "early warning" tests that can show potential problems, and how to choose doctors who are supportive of running and exercise. Consult your medical team on all medical issues. RUNNING UNTIL YOU'RE 100 has a lot of practical information for the "over 40" crowd.

Humans were designed for long distance running—and walking
In the Journal NATURE, November 2004, Daniel Lieberman (Harvard), and Dennis Bramble (Univ of Utah) state that fossil evidence shows that ancient man ran and walked long distances. These experts and others point to the ancient bio-mechanisms of the ankle, achilles, buttocks, and many other components which are forward motion exercise-specific adaptations. According to the extensive research of these scientists and others, one can say that humans were born to run/walk, that covering long distances was a survival activity, and that body and mind are designed to adapt to gentle and regular walking/running. Some experts believe that ancient human ancestors ran before they walked.

Exercise prolongs life
Living longer is related to the number of calories burned per week. Dr. Ralph Paffenbarger conducted a highly acclaimed and

comprehensive study for the US Public Health Service, started in the 1960s. Results have been published in the Journal of the American Medical Association, April 1995 (co-authored by Doctors Lee and Hsieh). The conclusion: as the amount of exercise increases, rates of death from all major causes are reduced. Those who exercise more can statistically predict that they will live longer than they would when sedentary or with minimal exertion. His extensive research has also shown that the more calories burned, the greater the benefit.

Exercise reduced death rate in women. This was the conclusion by Lissner et al, in the American Journal of Epidemiology (Jan 1996), from an extensive study of Swedish women. The researchers also found that reducing physical activity increased risk of death. Sherman et al found that the most active women exercisers cut their death rate by one third (American Heart Journal, Nov 1994).

Breast cancer reduced in females who regularly exercised during the childbearing years. This was reported in the Journal of the National Cancer Institute.

Colon cancer and GI hemorrhage decreased by regular exercise. Several studies show a 30% reduction of colon cancer among regular exercisers. Gastrointestinal hemorrhage research is reported by Pahor et al (JAMA Aug 1994)

Starting exercise after the age of 60 can lengthen life. Dr. Kenneth Cooper, founder and director of the Cooper Clinic and the Cooper Institute of Aerobic Research, has volumes of research on various aspects of this topic. Findings also reveal that men of all ages who exercise regularly experience a 60% reduction in heart attacks, while women show a 40% reduction.

At any age...

Older runners can improve faster than younger runners. "You can maintain a very high performance standard into the sixth or seventh decade of life", said Dr. Peter Jokl, British Journal of Sports

Medicine August 2004(reported on MSNBC.com). This study found that runners over 50 years old improved their times in the NYC Marathon more than runners in younger age groups.

Older runners reduced their risk of heart disease, as they increased weekly mileage. Research in the National Runners Health Study shows that as runners increase their weekly mileage, they experience a reduced ratio of total cholesterol to the "bad" LDL cholesterol. Higher mileage runners also reduce systolic blood pressure, while cutting down on waist and hip fat. The reduction in LDL among those running 40+ miles per week, represents a 29-30% reduction in heart attack risk.

Mental benefits

Better thinking: Spirduso (Physical Fitness, Aging, and Psychomotor Speed: a review in Journal of Gerontology 1980) found that those who regularly exercised performed better on tests of cognitive functioning.

Less depression, better attitude: Eysenck et al (Adv Behav Res Ther 1982) found that active folks were more likely to be better adjusted compared with sedentary individuals. Folkins et al (American Journal of Psychology 1981) showed that exercise improves self-confidence and self-esteem. Weyerer et al reported that patients who exercised and were given counseling did better than with counseling alone (Sports Medicine, Feb 1994). Blumenthal et al (Journal of Gerontology 1989) found that exercise training reduces depression, and Martinsen et al (British Medical Journal 1985) found exercise very effective in populations with major depression. Camancho et al (American Journal of Epidemiology 1991) found that newcomers to exercise were at no greater risk for depression than those who had exercised regularly.

Running and joint health

Running does not predispose joints to arthritis Dan Wnorowski, MD, has written a paper which reviews research on the effects of running and joint health. He believes that the "majority of the revelant literature during the past decade" on this topic finds little or no basis that running increases arthritis risk. Wnorowski goes on to say that a recent MRI study indicates that the prevalence of knee meniscus abnormalities in asymptomatic marathon runners is no different than sedentary controls.

"Running or jogging does not increase the risk of osteoarthritis even though traditionally we thought it was a disease of wear and tear." Dr. Fries, from his study

- "Studies have shown that joint nourishment is entirely based upon keeping joints in motion" Charles Jung, MD from Group Health Cooperative website.

- "We don't see marathon runners having more joint injuries than sedentary folks. Simply put, active people have less joint injury." P.Z. Pearce, MD   from Group Health Cooperative website.

- "Running offers up to 12 year's protection from onset of osteoarthritis" BBC website 16 Oct 2002

- "Painless running or other activities which are aerobic and make you fit help keep you vigorous for longer." Professor Jim Fries, Stanford University (commenting upon results of his research at Stanford on aging exercisers).

- "Inactivity was once thought to prevent arthritis and protect fragile arthritic joints from further damage. More recent research has demonstrated the opposite." Benjamin Ebert, MD, PH.D. as quoted in Dr. Larry Smith's website.

- "The notion that sports and recreational activities cause an inevitable wear on the joints just does not hold up when the scientific studies are evaluated. Few competitive, or recreational long distance runners suffer severe joint injuries..." Ross Hauser, M.D, and Marion Hauser M.S.R.D. as quoted in Dr. Larry Smith's website.

Older runners reported pain and disability only 25% as often as those who didn't run. A study conduced by Fries, et al

"Reasonably long-duration, high mileage running need not be associated with premature degenerative joint disease of the lower extremities." Panush et al, "Is Running Associated with Degenerative Joint Disease?"JAMA 1986. Subjects were at least 50 years old, mean # of years running: 12, mean weekly mileage 28.

No increase in degenerative joint disease in runners. "Competitive sports increase joint risk—but running risk is low". Lane, et al, "Risk of Osteoarthritis(OA) With Running and Aging: Five-Year Longitudinal Study". Studied runners 50-72 years old. Findings were similar to the conclusions of a study in 1989.

"Running seems to be devoid of adverse effects leading to knee degeneration, compared with other sports." Kujala et al, "Knee Osteoarthritis in Former Runners, Soccer Players, Weight Lifters, and Shooters" (Arthritis & Rheumatism, 1995)

"Runners averaging 66 years of age have not experienced accelerated development of radiographic OA (Osteo-Arthritis) of the knee compared with nonrunner controls" Lane et al, Journal of Rheumatology 1998.

"Older individuals with OA of the knees (not endstage) benefit from exercise." Ettinger et al, JAMA 1997.

"Little or no risk of OA with lifelong distance running" Konradsen et al, (AJSM 1990) studied a group that tends to abuse the orthopedic limits (former competitive runners) who ran 20-40 km per week for 40 years. Other interesting studies include Lane et al, JAMA 1989, Kujala et al, Arthritis & Rheumatism 1995.

Note: The American Heart Association has a wonderful document that details the varied and significant benefits from exercise, citing 107 research sources. You can search for this on the internet under "AHA Medical/Scientific Statement".

What Happens to Us as We Get "in Shape"

Humans are designed to improve their fitness and endurance

When we regularly run, many positive changes occur inside us. I believe that this is due to the way our bodies were adapted to the covering of long distances by our ancient ancestors. Before primitive man invented tools, survival depended upon moving feet and legs to the next food supply. The physical design and purpose of the of the human body is long distance walking and running, so it's natural for us to feel satisfaction after a run—we're going back to our roots.

Teamwork

When called into action, the heart, lungs, muscles, tendons, central nerve transmission, brain and blood system are all programmed to work as a team. The right brain intuitively solves problems, manages resources, and steers us toward the treasury of health benefits bestowed by running.

Each muscle is like a factory composed of thousands of muscle cells which do the work. Unlike some factory workers, these are passionate and dedicated team members ready to work 24/7 to keep us moving—even when we push them to exhaustion over and over again. Running, even in short amounts done slowly, calls them into action, stimulates them to improve, and serves to mold them into a team.

Among other important functions, your leg muscles help to pump blood back to the heart. By gradually extending the length of your long runs, you produce very fit muscle cells in the legs. Some cardiovascular experts who study the heart believe that the cumulative effect of endurance-trained leg muscle action reduces heart strain by pushing blood through the system.

Vital organs kept in shape by running

- *Heart:* Your heart is a muscle and responds positively to endurance exercise. A strong and effective heart pumps blood more effectively not only when you exercise. Heart specialists say that this "fit" heart is more resistant to heart disease.
- *Lungs* On our long runs, our lungs are stimulated to improve oxygen absorption, loading up the red blood cells for continuous delivery of oxygen to exercising muscles.
- *Endorphins* kill pain, make you feel good, Endorphins manage muscle pain and provide a positive lift to the spirit. This is why you feel good after a workout. Through managing your effort, you can enjoy the benefits during exercise.

Stress + rest = improvement

When you run a little farther than you've gone in the past month or so, the gentle stress breaks down the muscle cells, tendons, etc. This stimulates your body to rebuild, stronger than before, if you have enough rest afterward (usually 48 hours).

Looking inside the cell afterward, you'll see tears in the muscle cell membrane. The mitochondria (the energy processors inside the cell) are swollen. Glycogen (the energy supply needed for the first 15 minutes of exercise) is significantly reduced. There are waste products from exercise and even bits of muscle tissue and other residue from a hard effort. Sometimes, breaks in the blood vessels and arteries occur, with leakage of blood into the muscles. If you have only increased your distance by a mile or less (at a gentle pace for you) this damage can be repaired quickly.

You must have a slight breakdown of the muscles to stimulate improvements in the system. If you have rested well, and can look inside the cell again 2 days later, you'll see thicker cell membranes, which can handle more work without breaking down. The mitochondria have increased in size and number, so that they can process more energy next time. The damage to the blood system has been repaired. Waste has been removed. Over several months, after adapting to a continued series of small increases, more capilliaries (tiny fingers of the blood system) are produced. This improves and expands the delivery of oxygen and nutrients and provides a better withdrawal of waste products.

Beware of junk miles

Some beginners feel so good when they start a program that they "sneak in" a few miles on the days they should be resting. They often lie to themselves, assuming that this short distance isn't really tiring. But these short runs don't allow the muscles to recover before the next run.

Regularity

To maintain the adaptations, you must regularly exercise (about every 2-3 days). Waiting longer than this, will cause a slight loss in the muscle adaptations you have been developing, each day. The longer you wait, beyond 3 days, the harder it will be to start up again.

Difference between aerobic and anaerobic exercise

Aerobic means "in the presence of oxygen". Most walking and running sessions are done aerobically: slowly enough to be within your current capabilities, so that your muscles can get enough oxygen to process the energy in the cells (burning fat in most cases). The minimal waste products produced during aerobic exercise can be easily removed.

Anaerobic means exercising at a pace that is too fast or a distance that is too long for you, pushing you beyond your trained range. Your muscles can't get enough oxygen to burn the most efficient fuel (fat) so they shift to "stored sugar", called glycogen. The waste products from this fuel pile up quickly in the cells, tightening the muscles and causing you to breathe heavily. If you keep exercising anaerobically, you will have to slow down significantly or stop. Anaerobic exercise requires a longer recovery period, and often results in sore, painful muscles the next day.

What Do You Need to Get Started?

There are a growing number of "things" that can help make running easier: shoes, clothing, a training journal, watches, water belts, sun glasses, etc. The choice of bras is detailed in the second chapter on women's issues. As a running store owner myself, I'm very pleased that these items make exercise easier and more fun. But remember that top priority is to learn how to enjoy the exercise experience. In other words, don't load up on everything you could possibly need for the rest of your exercise life—until you know you like it (unless you're in my Phidippides store in Atlanta). Focus on finding shoes, clothing and equipment that makes you comfortable, and enhances your run.

Medical check

Check with your doctor's office before you start exercising. Just tell the doctor or head nurse that you plan to do a little jogging, building up to running with walk breaks, every other day. Almost every person will be given the green light. If your doctor recommends against this, ask why. Since there are so few people who have problems related to running with liberal walk breaks, I suggest that you get a second opinion if your doctor tells you not to exercise. The best medical advisor is one who wants you to regularly exercise, and will work with you to run if at all possible.

Heart disease and exercise

Running tends to offer some protection from cardiovascular disease. But more women exercisers die of heart disease than any other cause, and are susceptible to the same risk factors as sedentary people. Like most other citizens, exercisers at risk usually don't know they are at risk. We know of a number of runners who have suffered heart attacks and strokes who probably could have prevented them if they had taken a few simple tests. Some of these are listed below, but check with your doctor if you have any questions or concerns.

Risk factors—get checked if you have two of these—or one that your doctor notes as "significant"
- Family history
- Poor lifestyle habits earlier in life
- High fat/high cholesterol diet
- Have smoked—or still smoke
- Obese or severely overweight
- High blood pressure (Good to be under 135/85, better if under 125/75)
- High cholesterol (Good to be under 180, better if under 150)
- High blood sugar (Good to be under 100)

Tests can tell you if you are at risk
- Stress test—heart is monitored during a run that gradually increases in difficulty. This test will screen out some at risk, but many with real problems fall through the cracks.

- Cholesterol screening—A number that is below 180 is good, and below 150 is excellent. Ask your doctor about your individual situation and the variation between your HDL particles (better to have a higher percentage) and your LDL (particles that can cause problems).
- C reactive protein—has been an indicator of increased risk
- Heart scan—an electronic scan of the heart which shows calcification, and possible narrowing of arteries. A higher than normal reading does not mean blockage but may indicate the need for more tests.
- Radioactive dye test—very effective in locating specific blockages. Talk to your doctor about this.
- Carotid ultrasound test—helps to tell if you're at risk for stroke
- Ankle-brachial test—denotes plaque buildup in arteries throughout the body

None of these are foolproof. But by working with your cardiologist, you can increase your chance of living until the muscles just won't propel you further down the road.

Safety

Take charge by thinking ahead and being aware of your surroundings.
- Bring a shrill whistle with you
- In uncertain areas, bring pepper spray
- Bring a cell phone, and call someone if you feel threatened
- Wear an ID tag on your shoe
- Tell someone where you will be running, and when you should be back
- Use your instincts—turn around if you feel uneasy on a certain street
- Wear white and reflective clothing at night, and run where the streets are well lit
- Don't take chances in traffic—wait until the traffic is clear to cross the street
- Run facing traffic—and always have an escape route. Assume all drivers are crazy or drunk.

- When running with others, never assume that someone is looking ahead for your safety—it's your job!
- Best not to wear any device in your ear, but if you do, keep the sound as low as possible and one ear uncovered.
- If threatened, swing your elbow at the head of the attacker, put fingers in the eyes, kick in the groin

Shoes: the primary investment: usually less than $100 and more than $65

It's a good idea to spend a little time on the choice of a good running shoe. After all, shoes are one of two real pieces of equipment needed (bras are the second item). The correct shoe can make running easier, reducing blisters, foot fatigue and injuries. Get the best advice you can from the staff at the best running store in your area.

Clothing: comfort above all

The "clothing thermometer" at the end of this book will tell you what works for most runners at various temperatures. In the summer, you want to wear light, cool clothing. During cold weather, layers are the best strategy. As you get into longer sessions, you will find various outfits that make you feel better and motivate you to get in your workout even on bad weather days. It is also OK to give yourself a fashionable outfit as a "reward" for exercising regularly for several weeks.

A training journal

Your journal can organize your running as it motivates you. By using it to plan ahead and then later, to review mistakes, you take a major degree of control over your future. You'll find it reinforcing to write down what you did each day, and miss that reinforcement when you skip.

Where to run

The best place to start is in your neighborhood—especially if there are sidewalks. First priority is safety. Pick a course that is away from car traffic, and is in a safe area—where crime is unlikely. Variety can be very motivating.

Surface

With the selection of the right shoes for you, pavement should not give extra shock to the legs or body. A smooth surface dirt or gravel path is best for most people, but hard to find. Beware of an uneven surface, especially if you have weak ankles or foot problems.

Picking a running companion

Don't run with someone who is faster than you—unless he/she is fully comfortable slowing down to an easy pace—that is...comfortable for you. It is motivating to exercise with someone who will go slow enough so that you can talk. Share stories, jokes, problems if you wish, and you'll bond together in a very positive way. The friendships forged during the long sessions can be the strongest and longest lasting—if you're not huffing and puffing (or puking) from trying to maintain a pace that is too difficult.

Rewards

Rewards are important at all times. But they are crucial for most runners in the first 3-6 weeks. Be sensitive and provide rewards that will keep you motivated, and make the running experience a better one (more comfortable shoes, clothes, etc.)

Positive reinforcement works! Treating yourself to a smoothie after a workout, taking a cool dip in a pool, going out to a special restaurant after a longer one—all of these can reinforce the good habit you are establishing. In fact, you'll speed recovery by having a snack, within 30 minutes of the finish, one with about 200-300 calories, containing 80% carbohydrate and 20% protein. The products Accelerade and Endurox R4 are already formulated with this ratio for your convenience, and make good rewards.

An appointment on the calendar

Write down each of your weekly workouts, 2 weeks in advance, on your calendar. Sure you can change if you have to. But by getting the "appointment" secure, you can plan your day, and make it happen. Pretend that this is an appointment with your favorite relative, your boss, or your most important client, etc. Actually, you are your most important client!

Treadmills are just as good as streets

More and more walkers/runners are using treadmills for at least 50% of their runs/walks—particularly women who have small children. It is a fact that treadmills tend to tell you that you have gone further or faster than you really have (usually are not off by more than 10%). But if you exercise on a treadmill for the number of minutes assigned, at the effort level you are used to (no huffing and puffing), you will get close enough to the training effect you wish. To ensure that you have covered enough miles, feel free to add 10% to your assigned mileage.

Runing strollers

Strollers can give mothers more freedom to run/walk outside, with child or children. There are a number of quality products that make the ride smooth and reduce the effort of pushing one or two kids around. (Yes there are models designed for two.) Try several out, and ask around for used ones. You want one that will fold up and can be put in your car easily, is easy to steer, is comfortable for your child (children) and has a hand strap. Twenty-inch wheels (or larger) are generally recommended. Some running clubs and running stores try to match up used stroller-sellers, with buyers.

Usually no need to eat before exercise

Most runners/walkers don't need to eat before sessions that are less than about an hour and a half. The only exceptions are those with diabetes or severe blood sugar problems. Many exercisers feel better during a workout when they have enjoyed a cup of coffee about an hour before the start. Caffeine engages the central nervous system, which gets all of the systems needed for exercise up and running to capacity, very quickly. Don't take caffeine if you have heart rhythm problems or caffeine sensitivities.

If your blood sugar is low, which often occurs in the afternoon, it helps to have a snack of about 100-200 calories, about 30 minutes before exercise, that is composed of 80% carbohydrate and 20% protein. The Accelerade product has been very successful.

A Trip to the Running Store

"I couldn't believe the difference in my running when I found a running shoe designed for my feet"

Ask several runners or walkers, particularly those who have exercised for 10 years or more, about the running stores in your area. Pick a store that has a reputation for spending time with each customer to find a shoe that will best match the shape and function of the foot. Be prepared to spend at least 45 minutes in the store. Quality stores are often busy, and quality fitting takes time. Getting good advice can save your feet. Experienced and committed running shoe staff members match you up with shoes through a complex series of judgements based upon experience. I hear from runners about every week, who purchased a "great deal" but had to use it for lawn mowing because it wasn't designed for the way their feet moved during exercise.

Bring your most worn pair of shoes you own—walking or running

The pattern of wear on a well-used walking or running shoe reveals the way your foot functions, as "read" by a shoe expert.

A knowledgeable shoe store staff person can usually notice how your foot functions

…by watching you walk and run. This is a skill gained through the experience of fitting thousands of feet.

Give feedback

As you work with the person in the store you need to give feedback as to how the shoe fits and feels. You want the shoe to protect your foot while usually allowing the foot to go through a running/walking motion that is natural for you. Tell the staff person if there are pressure points or pains—or that it just doesn't feel right.

Reveal any injuries or foot problems

If you have had shin pain, or some joint issues (knee, hip, ankle) possibly caused by the "over-pronation" of your foot (see sidebar below) you may need a shoe that protects your foot from this excess motion. Try several shoes in the "stability" category to see which seems to feel best. If you need more support, you'll move to the "motion control" group.

Don't try to fix your foot if it isn't broken

Even if your foot rolls excessively one way or the other, you don't necessarily need to get an over-controlling shoe. Your feet and legs make many adjustments and adaptations which keep many runners injury free—even when they have extreme motions that are harmful to others.

Expensive shoes are often not the best for you

The most expensive shoes are usually not the best shoes for your feet. You cannot assume that high price will buy you extra protection from injury or more miles. At the price of some of the shoes, you might expect that they would do the running for you. They won't.

Go by fit and not the size noted on the shoe box

Most runners will fit best into a running shoe that is about 2 sizes larger than their street shoe. Be open to getting the best fit— regardless of what size you see on the running shoe box. Shoe experts can guide you here, also.

Extra room for your toes—about half an inch

Your foot tends to swell during the day, so it's best to fit your shoes after noontime. Be sure to stand up in the shoe during the fitting process to measure how much extra room you have in the toe region of the shoe. Pay attention to the longest of your feet, and leave at least half an inch.

Width issues

- Running shoes tend to be a bit wider than street shoes.
- Usually, the lacing can "snug up" the difference, if your foot is a bit narrower.
- The shoe shouldn't be laced too tight around your foot because the foot swells during running. On hot days, the average runner will move up one-half shoe size.
- In general, running shoes are designed to handle a certain amount of "looseness". But if you are getting blisters when wearing a loose shoe, snug the laces.
- Several shoe companies have some shoes in widths

Shoes for women

Women's shoes tend to be slightly narrower than those for men, and the heel is usually a bit smaller. The quality of the women's versions of major running shoe brands is equal to those of men. But about 25% of women runners have feet that can fit better into men's shoes. Usually the confusion comes in women who wear large sizes. The better running stores can help you make a choice in this area.

If the shoe color doesn't match your outfit, it's not the end of the world

I receive several emails every year concerning injuries that were produced by wearing the wrong shoe. Some of these are "fashion injuries" in which the runner picked a shoe only because the color matched the new outfit. Remember that there are no fashion police out there on the sidewalks or trails.

BREAKING IN A NEW SHOE

- Wear the new shoe around the house, for a few minutes each day for a week. If you stay on carpet, and the shoe doesn't fit correctly, you can exchange it at the store. But if you have put some wear (dirt, etc) on the shoe, few stores will take it back.

- In most cases you will find that the shoe feels comfortable enough to exercise immediately, but this is not a good idea. It is best to continue walking in the shoe, gradually allowing the foot to accommodate to the inner shoe construction: arch, heel area, ankle pads, and to make other adjustments. If you run/walk in the shoe too soon, blisters are often the result.

- If there are no rubbing issues on the foot when walking, you could walk in the new shoe for a gradually increasing amount for 2-4 days.

- On the first exercise session in the new shoe, just run about half a mile in the shoe. Put on your old shoes and continue.

- On each successive run, increase the amount done in the new shoe for 3-4 sessions. At this point, you will usually have the new shoe broken in.

HOW DO YOU KNOW WHEN IT'S TIME TO GET A NEW SHOE?

1. When you have been using a shoe for 3-4 weeks successfully, buy another pair of exactly the same model, make, size, etc. The reason for this: The shoe companies often make significant changes or discontinue shoe models (even successful ones) every 6-8 months.

2. Gradually break in the new pair as noted above.

3. After the shoe feels broken in, run the first half mile of one of your weekly workouts in the new shoe, then use the shoe that is already broken in.

4. On the "shoe break-in" day, gradually run a little more in the new shoe. Continue to do this only one day a week. Be sure to run in your old shoe for a comparison.

5. Several weeks later you will notice that the new shoe offers more bounce than the old one

6. When the old shoe doesn't offer the support you like, shift to the new pair. Don't wait until the old pair is "shot".

7. Start breaking in a third pair.

Note: There's more information on shoes and fitting in GALLOWAY'S BOOK ON RUNNING SECOND EDITION, and most of my other books listed at the end of this book.

#11

Getting Started

"As soon as you take responsibility for running three days a week, and making it fun, you become a successful runner."

Now is the time for beginners to get started. The strategy is simple: make sure that you enjoy exercise, and keep doing it for three weeks—then you can shift into the rest of the 6 month program in this book. A very high percentage of those who run for 6 months, are "hooked" for life.

You have a great deal of control over that part of life that revolves around exercise, if you choose to take charge. The way you schedule your runs, your rewards, and your challenges will significantly influence motivation and this will determine the number of energizing workouts you get in per week. But you also can control how good you will feel during each run and how quickly you will recover.

There is no need to ever experience pain in a running program. But this puts on you, the new exerciser, the responsibility of never making a big jump in the amount that you will do at one time. You can have fun when you run—every single day if you hold yourself back and don't spend all of the resources early.

A training journal can improve motivation. Flip through the journal, look ahead, and write down the three days a week you will run, each week for 2-3 weeks. Be sure to pick a time then the temperature is OK for you, and a segment of the day when you should have the time to exercise. Lock it in! When you write it down, you make a commitment to yourself and you're more likely to do it. Of course, you still have to get out the door and move your legs. If you wait until the spirit moves you, you will probably have many empty spaces in your training journal.

You must take charge of the little things that keep the schedule filled—such as the following:

- Spend a few minutes a week to plan your weekly sessions
- Reward yourself afterward
- Find a way to enjoy every run/walk
- Regularity is important for the body and the mind. When you have 3 exercise-free days in a row, between runs/walks, you start to lose some of your conditioning and adaptations.
- Every other day is a better exercise pattern than 2 or 3 days in a row—at the beginning of your training program. Having a day off between run/walks lets the leg muscles rebuild and rebound more quickly. You'll find yourself looking forward to the next one. Also, your mind and spirit are more likely to pull you out on your next session, if you schedule them every second day.
- You don't have to use a technical training journal. A common notebook or calendar can work just as well to help you take control over your success. Schedule your runs/walks as "appointments" with the most important person in your life (you), and make sure that you show up at each appointment.

Top priority: Enjoying the first three weeks

A high percentage of those who follow the schedule below for 3 weeks will continue for 6 months. So, follow the successful program below for the next 21 days. Stick to it—one day at a time— and have fun!

How to make it more "fun"

1. Run at a time of the day when the temperature is comfortable.
2. If the weather doesn't cooperate, have an indoor alternative: treadmill, indoor track, indoor space where walking/running is allowed, etc.
3 No huffing and puffing is allowed. Walk/run at a slow pace for 10-15 minutes, then ease into the speed that is comfortable for you—on that day. Back off the pace and walk more if needed.
4. As much as possible, pick a pleasing venue
5. Reward yourself afterward: a smoothie, another snack, etc., after each session. After 3 weeks, new shoes, new outfit, etc.

Once you've run for 6 months, you're hooked!

Most of those who continue for half a year develop a positive addiction to exercise—and a very high percentage continue for life. In this book you will receive a schedule that lasts for 6 months. You can break this up any way you wish. Some like to focus on one week at a time, others a month....while others 3-6 months. Do what is motivating for you. Right now, however, we will focus on the first week.

A special run each week...and each month

It helps most beginners to schedule a special session each week— in a scenic area or with a motivating person or group. Each month, plan to run in a local 5K or regional festive event. Don't think that these events are only for seasoned competitors. Most participants enter because they enjoy the experience, and want to wear the race T-shirt. Be sure to read the chapter on your first race.

Veteran walkers and runners, who've exercised for 20 years or more tend to have the following things in common:

- They enjoy most of the miles covered, almost every day
- They take extra days off to recover from aches, pains, and burnout
- They don't let themselves get stuck in a rut—but add variety, regularly
- They don't let 3 days go by without exercising—even a short session

Exercising with others is very motivating

Talk family members or co-workers into joining you. Having someone to share the walk/run will motivate you to get going, and keep you going. Weekly (or more frequent) sessions with parents, kids, spouse, co-workers, offer special time together that will enhance your relationship...and your life.

Your First Week
–How to Begin and Continue

Schedule:

Monday, Wednesday and Friday:

15 to 25 minutes:

- 5 min slow walk as a warm up,
- then, 5-10 minutes walking with short running segments,
- then 5-10 minutes of walking as a "warm down".

Tuesday, Thursday and Saturday: off

Sunday: Longer Run/Walk—increase as noted on the schedule

Venues: home, work, kid's activity area...

The easier it is to get out the door, the more likely you will exercise. The most common venues are the following:

1. In your neighborhood, before the rest of the family has awakened
2. At noon, from your worksite
3. After work before other family members have arrived—or with friends or family members
4. After dinner—with other family members (not recommended if you have trouble sleeping)
5. When you are waiting for someone. Soccer moms run around the practice field, for example.

A caffeine boost?

To get the central nervous system ready for exercise, many exercisers have a cup of coffee, tea, or diet drink, about an hour before. If your blood sugar level is low due to any reason (especially in the afternoon), eat about half of an energy bar or 100-200 calories of a sports drink—especially one that has about 20% protein—about 25-30 min before the start of the walk/run. If you have problems with caffeine, don't use it.

Your stride: whether walking or running

Keep your feet low to the ground, lightly touching—as in a "shuffle". Don't lift your knees. In general, make it easy on yourself. You want to get into a groove when moving forward so that you don't feel the muscles, feet, joints. This means that everything is working together within a range of motion for which you are designed. Slow and gentle running in short segments, produces few, if any, aches and pains. Long strides, however, will increase the chance of injury. For the first two months I recommend a pace that is so easy that you don't huff and puff even at the end.

The first run

1. Put on a comfortable pair of running shoes
2. Put on light, comfortable clothes—see "clothing thermometer" in this book

Note: Clothes don't have to be designed for exercise—just comfortable

3. Walk for 5 minutes at a very slow pace to warm the muscles up gently
4. If the legs are moving comfortably and naturally, move into the next segment which includes some running segments.
5. During each running segment, get into a smooth motion that feels very comfortable to you.
6. Do this for 5-10 minutes—no more (Beginning runners will alternate 5-10 seconds of running with 60 seconds of walking)
7. Walk slowly for 5-10 minutes as a "warm-down".
8. There are watches that can be programmed to beep at the beginning and end of a run segment. You can see some of these at www.JeffGalloway.com

Warm-up

By walking for 5 minutes, very slowly, you will gently move the tendons and ligaments through the necessary range of motion. At the same time, you'll send blood into the muscles, as you get the heart, lungs, circulation system ready for gentle exertion. Your nerve system can get into "synch" when you have at least 5 minutes of easy movement as a warm-up. If you need more minutes of slow walking, continue doing so.

What? No stretching?

That's right. I see no reason to stretch before a run, unless you have some unusual problem that has been helped by stretching. The Iliotibial band injury is one of these exceptions. I believe, after working with over 200,000 exercisers through the years that stretching causes many injuries, with no benefits for most.

Breathing—no huffing and puffing

Don't let the level of exertion get to the point that you must huff and puff. You want to be able to talk or sing, as you do your exercise. This is called the "talk test".

Warm down

Just walk easily for 5-10 minutes. It is important that you keep moving the legs slowly after the walk/run. Don't ever go right into the shower after a vigorous walk, and don't stand around immediately after exertion either. Standing after a workout can be very stressful on your heart.

The day after

The next day, after your first workout, take the day off from exercise. After a few weeks you will have the option to take a short walk on these "easy days" but let's work on recovery at the beginning.

The second run

Two days after your first run, it's your "workout day" again. As long as you have recovered quickly from the first day, repeat the same routine as the first time, but extend the length by 3-5 minutes. If you haven't fully recovered, walk very slowly the whole time—and keep your stride very short and gentle.

Alternate

Continue to run about every other day, with a day off between. As long as the legs and body are recovering, you could continue increasing the middle segment by an additional 3-5 minutes on each session until the total reaches 30 minutes—see the schedule that follows this chapter. The warm up and warm down periods can stay the same.

Regularity

....is extremely important during the first 8 weeks. On a very busy day, if it is your walk/run day, get in at least a 5-minute session.

Even this short exercise period will help to maintain most of the adaptations. Naturally it is better to do more than this, but 5 minutes is better than zero. If you wait 3 days between runs, you start to lose the adaptations, and your body complains a bit longer into each session. Getting into a habit is the most helpful way to make it past 3 weeks—a major stepping stone to fitness success.

Reward yourself!

After you have finished your first week of three sessions, congratulate yourself with a special exercise outfit, meal, trip to a scenic walk area, etc. Remember that rewards can be very powerful.

Congratulations! You're on your way!

#13

Training Programs for Beginning Runners

If you can settle into your running habit during the next three weeks—only 9 sessions—you have about an 80% chance of continuing to run for 6 months, according to my experience. The members of the "six month club" tend to continue as life-long exercisers. Here are some tips for your 21 day mission:

• Find a place in your schedule when you are very likely to have time to exercise. For most people this means getting up 30 minutes early. Go to bed 30 minutes early. But even if you don't, you should be fine with 30 minutes less sleep. The overwhelming response from exercisers I've worked with, who've initially said they couldn't live without those 30 minutes (but gave it a try), is.....they really had no problem. The vitality you gain from your gentle exercise session will energize the rest of your day.

- Get your spouse, significant other, friends, co-workers, etc., to be your support team. Promise that if you get through the next 3 weeks having done each of the runs (only 9 of them), that you will have a party for them, picnic, whatever. Pick supportive people who will email you, and will reinforce your exercise during and after the training.
- Have a friend or three who you can call, in case you have a low motivation day. Just the voice on the phone can usually get you out the door. Of course it is always better to have a positive and enthusiastic person in this role.
- It is best to also have a back-up time to run. The usual times for this are at noon or after work.
- While commuter traffic is high, get in your workout: some get to work very early, and others run immediately after work.
- If necessary, you can break up your running time into several segments: morning, lunch hour, after dinner.

Remember, no huffing and puffing!

WEEK 2

Mission: You are continuing to increase distance. On Sunday, pick a scenic place for your run. This week, during the second section, run for 5-15 seconds, then walk 1-2 minutes.

Mon	Tue	Wed	Thurs	Fri	Sat	Sun
15-18 min	Off	17-19 min	Off	19-21min	off	21-23 min

WEEK 3

Mission: You're really making progress now—getting up near the half-hour mark! On Saturday, ask some friends to go with you for the warm up and warm down—and have a picnic afterward. You've made it 3 weeks. Keep going, you have an easy week coming. The running segments can increase to 10-20 seconds of running, followed by 1-2 minutes of walking.

Mon	Tue	Wed	Thurs	Fri	Sat	Sun
Off	23-28min	off	25-27min	off	28-30 min	off

WEEK 4

Mission: Rest a bit. This is an easier week, to make sure the body catches up. You have earned this. Run for the same run-walk ratio as in week 3.

Mon	Tue	Wed	Thurs	Fri	Sat	Sun
20-22 min	off	20 min	off	25 min	off	22 min

You will do this! Just focus on each day, and make the little adjustments that you need to make. While you are doing your runs, you can plan your success party. If you pick the right people, you may have some converts and companions who will join you in your mission and start running with you!

"You've made it through the toughest part of the program, you only need to maintain momentum, now."

This program is designed for those who've finished the program for the first few weeks, listed above, and are ready to continue. This is a run-walk-run ™ program and you will gradually introduce your body to the running motion. If the amount of running is too much for you, drop back to a schedule that feels comfortable until you are ready to move on.

We will start adding a cadence drill each week after the first few weeks. You can move this drill to any day, but just try get it in. More than any other activity, cadence drills improve your running efficiency and ease of running, while you teach yourself to run faster. This is not a workout that "hurts". In fact, most runners say that the cadence segments infuse energy into a run—mentally and physically.

Cadence drill [on the Wednesdays designated by a *CD]
1. Warm up the usual way
2. After about 5-10 minutes, start your drill
3. Time yourself for 30 seconds and just count how many times your left foot touches. If you feel more comfortable with 10 or 20 seconds, just count for a segment of that amount.

4. Walk for 1-2 minutes and repeat, increasing the count by 1 or 2.
5. Repeat this 2-6 more times, attempting to increase by 1-2 on each
6. You are focusing on getting more counts. Don't try to run faster, but a slight increase might be the natural result
7. After the cadence drill, just finish out the time assigned for that day
8. Whatever time segment you choose (10, 15, or 20 seconds), stay with that amount

Run-Walk-Run ™ Training Program: Weeks 5-26

Mon	Tue	Wed	Thurs	Fri	Sat	Sun
Week 5—run 10-14 seconds/walk 1-2 minutes						
20 min Run-Walk	walk 22 min	20 min Run-Walk	walk 22 min	off	23 min Run-Walk	22 min Walk
Week 6—-run 10-14 seconds/walk 1-2 minutes						
22 min Run-Walk	walk 23 min	22 min	walk 23 min	off	26 min Run Walk	23 min Walk
Week 7—run 10-14 seconds/walk 1-2 minutes						
16 min Run-Walk	walk 18 min	16 min Run-walk	walk 18 min	off	20 min Run-Walk	20 min Walk
Week 8—run 12-16 seconds/walk 1-2 min						
24 min Run-Walk	walk 24 min	24 min Run-Walk	walk 24 min	off	29 min Run-Walk	24 min Walk
Week 9—run 12-16 seconds/walk 1-2 min						
25 min Run-Walk	walk 25 min	25 min Run-Walk	walk 25 min	off	32 min Run-Walk	25 min Walk
Week 10—run 12-16 seconds/walk 60-90 seconds						
20 min Run-Walk	walk 20 min	20 min Run-Walk	walk 20 min	off	24 min Run-Walk	20 min Walk
Week 11—run 14-18 seconds/walk 60-90sec						
26 min Run-Walk	walk 26 min	26 min Run-Walk	walk 26 min	off	34 min Run-Walk	26 min Walk
Week 12—run 14-18 seconds/walk 60-90 sec						
27 min Run-Walk	walk 27 min	27 min Run-Walk	walk 27 min	off	36 min Run-Walk	27 min Walk

Week 13—run 14-18 seconds/walk 55-90 seconds

20 min Run-Walk	walk 20 min	20 min Run-Walk	walk 20 min	off	29 min Run-Walk	20 min Walk

Week 14—run 16-18 seconds/walk 55-80 sec

28 min Run-Walk	walk 28 min	28 min *CD Run-Walk	walk 28 min	off	38 min Run-Walk	28 min Walk

Week 15—run 16-18 seconds/walk 50-80 sec

29 min Run-Walk	walk 29 min	29 min* *CD Run-Walk	walk 29 min	off	40 min Run-Walk	29 min Walk

Week 16—run 16-18 seconds/walk 50-75 sec

20 min Run-Walk	alk 20 min	22 min* *CD Run-Walk	walk 20 min	off	31 min Run-Walk	20 min Walk

Week 17—run 18-20 seconds/walk 45-75 sec

30 min Run-Walk	walk 30 min	30 min *CD Run-Walk	walk 30 min	off	42 min Run-Walk	30 min Walk

Week 18—run 18-20 seconds/walk 45-70 sec

30 min Run-Walk	walk 30 min	30 min *CD Run-Walk	walk 30 min	off	44 min Run-Walk	30 min Walk

Week 19—run 18-20 seconds/walk 40-70 sec

20 min Run-Walk	walk 20 min	22 min *CD Run-Walk	walk 20 min	off	33 min Run-Walk	20 min Walk

Week 20—run 20-22 seconds/walk 40-65 sec

30 min Run-Walk	walk 30 min	30 min *CD Run-Walk	walk 30 min	off	46 min Run-Walk	30 min Walk

Week 21—run 20-22 seconds/walk 35-65 sec

30 min Run-Walk	walk 30 min	30 min *CD Run-Walk	walk 30 min	off	48 min Run-Walk	30 min Walk

Week 22—run 20-22 seconds/walk 35-60 sec

22 min	walk 22 min	22 min *CD	walk 22 min	off	35 min	22 min
Run-Walk		Run-Walk			Run-Walk	Walk

Week 23—run 22-24 seconds/walk 30-60 sec

30 min	walk 30 min	30 min *CD	walk 30 min	off	50 min	30 min
Run-Walk		Run-Walk			Run-Walk	Walk

Week 24—run 22-24 seconds/walk 30-60 sec

30 min	walk 30 min	30 min *CD	walk 30 min	off	52 min	30 min
Run-Walk		Run-Walk			Run-Walk	Walk

Week 25—run 22-24 seconds/walk 25-60 sec

22 min	walk 22 min	22 min *CD	walk 22 min	off	37 min	22 min
Run-Walk		Run-Walk			Run-Walk	Walk

Week 26—run 24-26 seconds/walk 25-60 sec

30 min	walk 30 min	30 min *CD	walk 30 min	off	54 min	30 min
Run-Walk		Run-Walk			Run-Walk	Walk

Note: continue after this point, alternating week # 25 and Week # 26

Fat Burning Program (weeks 5-26)

The time spent walking increases significantly in this program, so keep the pace very slow. The idea is to keep from huffing and puffing as you increase the distance covered. You can break up your exercise into two sessions if you wish, with the exception of the long run on the weekend—which should be done in one continuous workout. See the fat burning chapter for more details on how additional miles of easy exercise promotes fat burning.

Mon	Tue	Wed	Thursday	Fri	Sat	Sun
Week 5—run 10-12 seconds/walk 1-2 minutes						
30 min Run-Walk	walk 35 min	30 min Run-Walk	walk 35 min	off	33 min Run-Walk	30min Walk
Week 6—-run 10-12 seconds/walk 1-2 minutes						
33 min Run-Walk	walk 35 min	32 min Run-Walk	walk 35 min	off	36 min Run Walk	33 min Walk
Week 7—run 10-12 seconds/walk 1-2 minutes						
23 min Run-Walk	walk 25 min	23 min Run-walk	walk 25 min	off	30 min Run-Walk	25 min Walk
Week 8—run 12-14 seconds/walk 1-2 min						
33 min Run-Walk	walk 38 min	33 min Run-Walk	walk 38 min	off	40 min Run-Walk	30 min Walk
Week 9—run 12-14 seconds/walk 1-2 min						
33 min Run-Walk	walk 38 min	33 min Run-Walk	walk 38 min	off	43 min Run-Walk	30 min Walk
Week 10—run 12-14 seconds/walk 1-2 min						
23 min Run-Walk	walk 25 min	23 min Run-Walk	walk 30 min	off	33 min Run-Walk	25 min Walk
Week 11—run 14-16 seconds/walk 1-2 min						
35 min Run-Walk	walk 40 min	35 min Run-Walk	walk 40 min	off	46 min Run-Walk	32 min Walk
Week 12—run 14-16 seconds/walk 1-2 min						
35 min Run-Walk	walk 40 min	35 min Run-Walk	walk 40 min	off	49 min Run-Walk	32 min Walk

Week 13—run 14-16 seconds/walk 1-2 min

25 min Run-Walk	walk 40 min	25 min Run-Walk	walk 40 min	off	36 min Run-Walk	25 min Walk

Week 14—run 14-18 seconds/walk 1-2 min

36 min Run-Walk	walk 44 min	36 min Run-Walk	walk 44 min	off	51 min Run-Walk	33 min Walk

Week 15—run 14-18 sec/walk 1-2 min

36 min Run-Walk	walk 44 min	36 min Run-Walk	walk 44 min	off	54 min Run-Walk	33 min Walk

Week 16—run 14-18 seconds/walk1-2 min

25 min Run-Walk	walk 35 min	25 min Run-Walk	walk 35 min	off	39 min Run-Walk	25 min Walk

Week 17—run 14-18 seconds/walk1-2 min

37 min Run-Walk	walk 48 min	37 min Run-Walk	walk 48 min	off	57 min Run-Walk	36 min Walk

Week 18—run 15-20 seconds/walk 1-2 min

37 min Run-Walk	walk 48 min	37 min Run-Walk	walk 48 min	off	60 min Run-Walk	36 min Walk

Week 19—run 15-20 seconds/walk 1-2 min

25 min Run-Walk	walk 38 min	25 min Run-Walk	walk 38 min	off	42 min Run-Walk	25 min Walk

Week 20—run 15-20 seconds/walk1-2 min

38 min Run-Walk	walk 52 min	38 min Run-Walk	walk 52 min	off	60 min Run-Walk	38 min Walk

Week 21—run 15-20 seconds/walk 1-2 min

38 min Run-Walk	walk 52 min	38 min Run-Walk	walk 52 min	off	60 min Run-Walk	38 min Walk

Week 22—run 15-20 seconds/walk 1-2 min

25 min Run-Walk	walk 40 min	25 min Run-Walk	walk 40 min	off	45 min Run-Walk	25 min Walk

Week 23—run 15-20 seconds/walk1-2 min

40 min Run-Walk	walk 56 min	40 min Run-Walk	walk 56 min	off	60 min Run-Walk	40 min Walk

Week 24—run 15-20 seconds/walk 1-2 min

| 40 min
Run-Walk | walk 56 min | 40 min
Run-Walk | walk 56 min | off | 60 min
Run-Walk | 40 min
Walk |

Week 25—run 15-20 seconds/walk 1-2 min

| 25 min
Run-Walk | walk 42 min | 25 min
Run-Walk | walk 42 min | off | 45 min
Run-Walk | 25 min
Walk |

Week 26—run 15-20 seconds/walk 1-2 min

| 40 min
Run-Walk | walk 60 min | 40 min
Run-Walk | walk 60 min | off | 60 min
Run-Walk | 40 min
Walk |

The Galloway Run-Walk-Run™ Method

"The scheduled use of walk breaks gives each runner control over fatigue and running enjoyment."

One of the wonderful aspects of running is that there is no definition of a "runner" that you must live up to. There are also no rules that you must follow as you do your daily run. You are the captain of your running ship and it is you who determines how far, how fast, how much you will run, walk, etc. While you will hear many opinions on this, running has always been a freestyle type of activity where each individual is empowered to mix and match the many variables and come out with the running experience that he or she chooses. Walking is the most important component for the first time runner, and can even give the veteran a chance to improve time. Here's how it works.

Walk before you get tired

Most of us, even when untrained, can walk for several miles before fatigue sets in, because walking is an activity that we are bio-engineered to do for hours. Running is more work, because you have to lift your body off the ground and then absorb the shock of the landing, over and over. This is why the continuous use of the running muscles will produce fatigue, aches, and pains much more quickly. If you insert a walk break into a run before your running muscles start to get tired, you allow the muscle to recover instantly—increasing your capacity for exercise while reducing the chance of next-day soreness. I've used this method successfully in training over 200,000 runners to reach their goals.

The "method" part involves having a strategy. By using a ratio of running and walking, listed below, you will manage your fatigue. Using this fatigue-reduction tool early, will save muscle resources and bestow the mental confidence to cope with any challenges that may come later. Even when you don't need the extra muscle strength and resiliency bestowed by the method, you will feel better during and after your run, and finish knowing that you could have gone further.

In your 6-month training program, you will be primarily walking at first. By inserting short segments of running, followed by longer walk breaks, your muscles adapt to running, without getting overwhelmed. As you improve your running ability, you will reach a point where you can set the ratio of running and walking—for that day.

"The run-walk method is very simple: you run for a short segment and then take a walk break, and keep repeating this pattern."

Walk breaks allow you to take control over fatigue in advance, so that you can enjoy every run. By taking them early and often you can feel strong, even after a run that is very long for you. Beginners will alternate very short run segments with short walks. Even elite runners find that walk breaks on long runs allow them to recover faster. There is no need to reach the end of a run, feeling exhausted—if you insert enough walk breaks, for you, on that day.

Walk breaks....

- give you control over your level of fatigue

- erase fatigue

- push back your tiredness "wall"

- allow for endorphins to collect during each walk break—you feel good!

- break up the distance into manageable units. ("one more minute until a walk break")

- speed recovery

- reduce the chance of aches, pains and injury

- allow you to feel good afterward—doing what you need to do without debilitating fatigue

- give you all of the endurance of the distance of each session—without the pain

- allow older runners to recover fast, and feel as good or better than the younger days

A short and gentle walking stride

It's better to walk slowly, with a short stride. There has been some irritation of the shins when runners or walkers maintain a stride that is too long. Relax and enjoy the walk.

No need to ever eliminate the walk breaks

Some beginners assume that they must work toward the day when they don't have to take any walk breaks at all. This is up to the individual, but is not recommended. Remember that you decide what ratio of run-walk-run to use. There is no rule that requires you to run any ratio of run-walk on any given day. I suggest that you adjust the ratio to how you feel.

I've run for about 50 years, and enjoy running more than ever because of walk breaks. Each run I take energizes my day. I would not be able to run almost every day if I didn't insert the walk breaks early and often. I start most runs taking a short walk break every minute.

How to keep track of the walk breaks

There are several watches which can be set to beep when it's time to walk, and then beep again when it's time to start up again. Check our website (www.jeffgalloway.com) or a good running store for advice in this area.

Why Does Your Body Want to Hold onto Fat?

Fat is our biological insurance policy against disaster. It is the fuel your body can use in case of starvation, sickness, injury to the digestive system, etc. We are genetically programmed to hold on to a certain amount of fat and this "set" amount is programmed to increase every year or so. I've spent years looking into this topic, and talking to experts in the field. This chapter will explain my beliefs about the process to help you gain more control over your fat percentage, based upon your needs and goals.

Many people start running to burn fat. Indeed, my run-walk-run™ method will tend to keep runners in a comfortable fat-burning mode longer than any other training method I know. Walk breaks and shuffle breaks not only help you enjoy endurance exercise so you can do more of it. These breaks give you control over the level of exertion, which can help you sustain fat burning for as long as you wish. When the body is conditioned for fat burning, it prefers this as fuel, because of the small amount of waste product produced.

Successful fat burners do three things:
1. Understand the process by reading this chapter and other sources
2. Establish a system to manage the eating (income) side of the equation
3. Set up a behavioral plan to burn fat, including lifestyle and exercise

How does fat accumulate?

When you eat some fat during a snack or a meal, you might as well put it into a syringe and inject it into your stomach or thigh. A gram of fat eaten is a gram of fat processed and put into the fat storage areas on your body. In addition, when you eat more calories than you need during a day from protein (fish, chicken, beef, tofu) and carbohydrate (breads, fruits, vegetables, sugar), the excess is converted into fat and stored.

Fat for survival

More than a million years of evolution have programmed your body to hold on to the fat you have stored because of a powerful principle: survival of the species. Before humans understood disease and prevention, they were susceptible to sweeping infections. Even mild diseases and flu wiped out a significant percentage of the population each year in primitive times. Those who had above-average fat stores survived periods of starvation and sickness, and passed on the fat accumulation adaptation to their children.

The powerful 'set point'

The set point is a biologically engineered survival mechanism that evolved to help us survive periods of forced calorie reduction. While it does seem possible to adjust it, you are going into battle against fat-storage processes that have been in place for over a million years. By understanding set point, you can set realistic goals for fat management—and at least reduce the increase.

Fat level is set in early 20s

Many experts agree that by about the age of 25 we have accumulated a level of fat that the body intuitively marks as it's lowest level. This "set point" is programmed to increase a little each year. The amount of increase is so small when we are young, that we usually don't realize that we're adding it—until about 10 years later, when it's time to go to a class reunion, etc.

Humans are supposed to carry around fat. But your set point does too good a job, continuing to add to the percentage each year, every year. And the amount of increase seems to be significantly greater as we get older. Even when you've had a year when stress or illness prevented the usual increase, the set point makes up by increasing appetite during the following year or two. Go ahead, shout "Unfair!" as loud as you wish. Your set point doesn't argue, it just makes another deposit. Exercise may help you lower the set point...so hold onto your hope.

Men and women deposit fat differently

While men tend to deposit fat on the surface of the skin, women (particularly in their 20s and 30s) fill up internal storage areas first. Most women will acknowledge that their weight is rising slightly year by year, but aren't concerned because there is no noticeable fat increase on the surface. This is why the "pinch test" is not always a good way to monitor fat buildup.

A common woman's complaint in the 30s or early 40s is the following: "My body has betrayed me—just during the past year I've been adding fat." In fact, fat has been deposited at a fairly consistent rate but hidden from view for many years. With many women, it is only when the internal fat storage areas are filled that they notice surface fat buildup.

Men find it easier to burn fat than women

When men start running regularly, many lose fat and weight for several months. Probably related to biological issues and primitive protections for mothers, women have a harder time burning it off. The reality is that you are ahead of the others in our society....even if you are maintaining the same weight. Because of the set point, one would expect an average 45-year-old woman in the US to gain

3-4 pounds a year. Running commonly allows women to hold the set point steady for years, and this is a victory. In other words, the set point may be controlled even if you are holding at the same weight, year to year.

Diets don't work because of the "starvation reflex"

We are certainly capable lowering food intake for days, weeks and months to lower fat levels and weight. This is a form of starvation and the set point has a long-term memory. Let's say that we lose that 10 pounds during the 2 months before the class reunion. Then, when you stop the diet, you'll experience a starvation reflex: a slight increase in appetite and hunger, over weeks and months until the fat accumulated on your body is higher that it was before the diet. It's a fact that almost all of those who lose fat on a diet put more pounds back within months of diet termination.

Waiting too long to eat triggers the starvation reflex

When you wait more than 3 hours without eating something, your set point organism senses that you may be going into a period of starvation. The longer you wait to eat, the more you will feel these three effects of the starvation reflex:

1. A reduction in your metabolism rate. Imagine an internal voice saying something like this: "if this person is going to start depriving me of food I had better tune down the metabolism rate to conserve resources". A slower metabolism means that you have no energy to exercise or move around—you feel lethargic, drowsy, and unmotivated in general.

2. An increase in the fat-depositing enzymes. The longer you wait to eat something, the more enzymes you will have, and the more fat will be actually deposited from your next meal.

3. Your appetite increases. The longer you wait to eat, the more likely it is that, for the next few meals, you will have an increased appetite: You're still hungry after a normal meal.

True ice cream confessions (from Jeff)

Barb and I used to like a particular type of ice cream so much that we ate a quart or more of it several nights a week. It was the reward we gave ourselves for reaching exercise goals for that day. Then, on a fateful New Year's day, we decided to eliminate the chocolate chip mint ice cream from our diet—after more than 10 years of enjoyment. We were successful for 2 years. A leftover box after a birthday party got us re-started on the habit, and we even increased our intake over what it had been before—due to having deprived ourselves.

You can "starve" yourself of a food that you dearly love for an extended period of time. But at some time in the future, when the food is around and no one else is.....you will tend to over-consume that food. Jeff's correction for this problem was the following:

1. I made a contract with myself: I could have a little of it whenever I wanted—while promising to be "reasonable".
2. Setting a goal of enjoying one bowl a week, 5 years from now
3. Four years from now, enjoying a bowl every 5 days
4. Three years from now, a bowl every 4 days
5. Learning to enjoy healthy sweet things, like fruit salads, energy bars, etc., as replacements.

It worked! I hardly ever eat any ice cream...but sometimes enjoy a bowl if I want. This is purely for medicinal reasons, you understand.

Low carb diets can be a scam

Low carb diets produce, primarily, a water weight loss—not a fat loss. The lack of sufficient carbohydrate causes a relatively quick loss of 10-25 pounds due to not restocking the glycogen (fuel stored in the muscle that is needed for exercise) and water to service the glycogen. The fat and extra protein in low carb diets usually adds fat to the body during the low carb diet, while the water weight loss is registered by the scales. When the dieter goes back to eating carbohydrate again, the water and glycogen weight returns and the added fat is then noticed with a weight gain.

This is a type of starvation diet. I've heard from countless low carb victims who admit that while they were on the diet, their psychological deprivation of carbs produced a significant rebound effect when they began eating them again. The cravings for bread, pastries, french fries, soft drinks, and other pound-adding foods, increased for months after they went off the diet. The weight goes back on, and on, and on.

Like so many diets, the low-carb diet reduces metabolism rate. This means that you're not burning the usual number of calories each day. When you return to eating a regular diet you will not have a "metabolism furnace" to burn up the increased calories.

Lowering the set point

Your body has a wonderful ability to adapt to the regular activities that you do. It also tries to avoid stress. In the next chapter we will talk about how to condition your muscles to be fat burning furnaces. Once you get them into shape to do this, you can move into a fat burning lifestyle. Lowering the set point is more complex, but possible—when you are regularly putting certain types of manageable stress on your system.

Endurance running causes a body temperature increase that can stimulate fat burnoff

Running slowly, with liberal walk breaks, can allow you to continue for 45 + minutes, increasing core body temperature. By creating this "artificial fever" you put a heat stress on the system, which your internal monitors would like to reduce. Since body fat acts like a blanket in maintaining this "fever", the body's intuitive, long-term solution is to gradually reduce the size of the fat blanket around you—lowering the set point. Three sessions a week, above 45 minutes each, are recommended. It helps if one of those sessions is 90 minutes or more.

Cross-training for fat burning

To maintain a regular dose of set-point lowering stress, while minimizing orthopedic stress, cross-training can help. The best activities are those that raise core body temperature, use a lot of muscle cells and can be continued comfortably for more than 45 minutes. Cross-training is done on days when you don't run. Swimming is not a good fat-burning exercise. The water absorbs temperature buildup, and therefore core body temperature doesn't rise significantly.

Good fat burning exercises
- Nordic track
- Walking
- Elliptical
- Rowing
- Exercise cycle

BMI can monitor fat level

What is the BMI? It is a simple computation of your "body mass index" using current weight and height. This has become the basic test to determine whether someone is overweight or obese. You can use the figure gained in this computation to track progress.

Adult BMI formula:

Inches/pounds: (weight in pounds) divided by (height in inches, squared) times 703
Example: 100-pound person that is 5 feet tall—100 divided by 3600 x 703 = 19.52 BMI
Example: 200-pound person that is 5 feet tall—200 divided by 3600 x 703 = 39.05

Meters/kilograms: (weight in kilograms) divided by (height in meters, squared)
Example: 100 kilogram-person that is 2 meters tall—100 divided by 4 = 25
Example: 160 kilogram-person that is 2 meters tall—160 divided by 4 = 40

Adults with a BMI of 25 to 29.9 are considered "overweight". When the BMI exceeds 30, the classification changes to obese.

#16

Why Some People
Burn a Lot More Fat....

Without losing a pound, if you run regularly you'll receive a series
of significant health benefits. Studies at the Cooper Clinic, founded
by Dr. Kenneth Cooper in Dallas TX, and other organizations, have
shown that even obese people lower their risk factors for heart
disease when they exercise regularly. According to a spokesperson,
the trend in the research shows that obese people who exercise
enough can have a significantly lower risk of heart disease and
cancer than thin people who don't exercise.

Slow, aerobic running is one of the very best ways to burn fat. But most runners, during their first year, usually hold their own, showing no weight loss. This is actually a victory over the set point. First, you are avoiding the average set-point-inspired increase of 2-4 pounds a year. But runners are actually burning fat by maintaining weight. How can this be? Read on.

As you run, your body stores more glycogen and water, all over the body, to process energy, and cool you off. Your blood volume also increases. All of these internal changes help you exercise better, but they cause a weight gain (not a fat gain). If your weight is the same a year after starting regular exercise, you have burned off several pounds of fat. Don't let the scales drive you crazy.

Long-term fat burnoff requires some personal responsibility. If you assume management of your eating and sufficient running each week, you will tend to keep the fat from accumulating. A seldom-noticed side effect of running is that runners tend to stay more active all day long. Once you get into the habit of getting out of your chair, regularly, you will be amazed at how many steps you will take per day, and how much better you feel.

Aerobic running burns fat

Oxygen is needed to burn fat. Therefore running at an easy pace, with walk breaks, will keep you in the aerobic, or "fat burning" zone. When you run too fast for that day and your muscles can't get enough oxygen, you will huff and puff (you're anaerobic). This is the sign that you are building up an oxygen debt. Without oxygen, the muscles will burn stored glycogen, which produces a high amount of waste product. This increases fatigue rapidly, and results in a burning and tightness in the muscles. If you want to maximize fat burning, you should slow down at the first sign of huffing, to get back into the fat-burning zone.

Sugar-burning during the first 15 minutes of exercise

Glycogen is the quick access fuel your body uses during the first quarter-hour of exercise. Those who don't exercise longer than 15 minutes will not get into fat burning, and won't train their muscles to burn this fuel. But if you have been depriving yourself of carbohydrates, as when on a low-carb diet, the fuel is low and you'll struggle during this warmup period.

Glycogen produces a high amount of waste product—mostly lactic acid. If you move slowly, with more walking, there can be no significant buildup. Even when the pace feels slow, if you are huffing and puffing within the first 10 minutes, you have been going too fast, for you, on that day. When in doubt, extend your slow walking at the beginning.

From 15 minutes to 45 minutes you will transition into fat burning If you are exercising within your capabilities, 15 minutes into your workout your body starts to break down body fat, and use it as fuel. Fat is actually a more efficient fuel, producing less waste product. This transition continues for the next 30 minutes or so. By the time you've been exercising within your capabilities for 45-50 minutes, you will be burning mostly fat—if the muscles are trained to do this. With lots of walking, and a slow pace, almost anyone can work up to three sessions of 45 minutes each.

Three sessions a week, in the fat burn zone

Even the most un-trained muscles that have only burned glycogen for 50 years can be trained to burn fat under two conditions:
- Get into the fat-burning zone 3 times a week (45 + min a week)
- Do this regularly: 3 times a week. (best to have no more than two days between sessions)

One session a week beyond 90 minutes

The endurance session is designed to keep you in the fat burn zone for an extended period. For best results, this should be done every week, and should increase gradually to around 90 minutes. If you don't have time for a 90-minute session, shoot for 60 minutes.

"By running/walking for 90 + minutes, one time each week, the leg muscles become fat burners. Over time, this means that you have thousands of muscle cells that are burning more fat 24/7, even when you are sitting around at your desk and sleeping at night."

Walk breaks allow you to go farther without getting tired

This pushes you into the fat burn zone while allowing for a quick recovery of the muscles. For fat-burning purposes, it is best to walk liberally from the beginning of a run, and walk more often. The number of calories you burn is based upon the number of miles covered. Walk breaks allow you to cover more distance each day, without tiring yourself. By lowering the exertion level, you will stay in the fat burning zone longer—usually for the whole session. When in doubt, it's best to insert more walk breaks and slow down the running pace.

Fat Burning Training:
for the Rest of Your Life

The long runs or walks will help to transform thousands of muscle cells into fat-burning furnaces. By keeping the pace slow, and by inserting walk or shuffle breaks into every exercise session, you can avoid aches, pains and injuries. You'll also stay in the fat-burning zone. A more gentle pace allows you to increase distance covered each week, significantly increasing the amount of calories burned.

10,000 or more steps a day (total of walking and running)

A pedometer, or step counter, can rev-up your fat-burning. As you check your count, you have an incentive and a reinforcement for adding extra steps to your day. It also gives you a sense of control over your actual calorie burnoff. Once you get into the goal of taking more than 10,000 steps a day in your everyday activities, you find yourself getting out of your chair more often, parking farther away from the supermarket, walking around the kid's playground, etc. In general, you learn how to move around instead of wait around.

These devices are usually about one inch square, and clip onto your belt, pocket or waistband. The simpler models just count steps and this is all you need. Other models compute miles and calories. I recommend getting one from a quality manufacturer. When tested, some of the really inexpensive ones registered 3-4 times as many steps as the quality products did—walking exactly the same course.

Your first goal is to gradually increase the daily step count to 10,000 by adding steps at home, at work, shopping, waiting for kids, etc., when you combine running and walking (or walking only). You will find many pockets of time during the day when you are just sitting or standing. When you use these to add steps to your day, you burn fat and feel better. You become a more active and energetic person.

About dinnertime you should do a "step check". If you haven't acquired your 10,000, walk around the block a few extra times after dinner—or add to the total over the next few days. You don't have to stop with these figures. As you get into it, you'll find many more opportunities to walk....and burn. We regularly hear from women who initially have trouble getting in 5,000 steps. After 3 months they are exceeding 10,000, and a year later are averaging 15,000 with less weight on the body.

Up to 65 pounds of fat....gone during a year

Depending upon how many times you do the following each week, you have some significant opportunities for burning fat each day. These are easy movements that don't produce tiredness, aches or pains, but at the end of the year—it really adds up:

Lbs per year	Activity
1-2 pounds	taking the stairs instead of the elevator
2-14 pounds	getting out of your chair at work to walk down the hall
1-10 pounds	walking around instead of waiting: for a child, spouse, meeting, airplane, etc

1-5 pounds	getting off the couch to move around the house (but not to get potato chips)
1-2 pounds	parking farther away from the supermarket, mall, etc
1-3 pounds	parking farther away from your work
2-4 pounds	walking around the kids playground, practice field (chasing the kids)
2-4 pounds	walking up and down the concourse as you wait for your next flight
3-9 pounds	walking the dog each day
2-4 pounds	walking a couple of times around the block after supper
2-4 pounds	walking a couple of times around the block during lunch hour at work
2-4 pounds	walking an extra loop around the mall, supermarket, etc. to look for bargains (this last one could be expensive when at the mall)

Total: 20-65 pounds a year

15 more pounds burned each year from adding a few extra miles a day

By using "dead time" when you can't do anything else, you can add to your fat-burning without feeling extra fatigue:

• Slow down and go one more mile on each run
• Walk a mile at lunchtime
• Jog a mile (walk 1.5-2 miles) before dinner, or afterward

 # 18

The Income Side of the Equation

Gaining control over your calorie intake is crucial for body fat reduction. Runners often complain that while they have increased mileage, and faithfully done cross-training workouts, they are not losing weight. In every case, when I have questioned them, each did not have a handle on the income side of the calorie ledger. When these individuals went through the drill of quantifying, each was eating more than they thought. Below you will find ways to cut 10 or more pounds out of your diet—without starving yourself. But even if you hold your intake as it is, you can burn fat pounds by using the non-strenuous exercise additions mentioned in the last chapter. When you're increasing up to 10,000 steps a day, holding calorie intake level produces a fat-burning victory.

Websites tell you calorie balance and nutrient balance

The best tool I've found for managing your food intake is a good website or software program. There are a number of these that will help to balance your calorie totals (calories burned vs. calories eaten). Most of these ask you to log in your exercise for the day, and what you eat. After dinner, you can retrieve an accounting of calories, and of nutrients. If you are low on certain vitamins or minerals, protein, etc., you can eat food or a vitamin pill. Some programs will tell vegetarians whether they have received enough complete protein, since this nutrient is harder to put together from vegetable sources. If you haven't received enough of some nutrient, you can do something about it the next day to make up the deficit. If you ate too many calories, walk after dinner or boost tomorrow's workouts, or reduce the calories, or all of the above.

I don't recommend letting any website control your nutritional life until the end of your days. At first, it helps to use it every day for 1-2 weeks. During this time, you'll see patterns and note where you tend to need supplementation or reductions. The most common offenders are simple carbohydrates, fat grams or foods like alcohol that are "calorie dense" and don't leave you satisfied. After you feel you have a good handle on what you're eating, do a spot check during 2-3 days, every 2-3 weeks or so. Some folks need more spot checks than others. If you're more motivated to eat the right foods and quantities by logging in every day, go for it.

For a list of the recommended websites, see my website: ***www.jeff-galloway.com.*** Try several out before you decide.

A portion of most foods is about the size of a fist

Portion control—through logging your food intake

Whether you use a website or not, a very productive drill is that of logging what you eat every day, for a week. Bring a little notepad, and a small scale if you need it, to every meal, and also record the snacks. As people log in, they are almost always surprised at the number of calories and fat grams they are eating. Many foods have the fat so well disguised that you don't realize how much you are eating.

After doing this drill for several days you start to adjust the amount of food, and the components of your snacks or meals. You are gaining control! Many exercisers have said that they resented the first week of logging in, but it became fairly routine after that. Once you get used to doing this, you become aware of what you will be putting in your mouth, are taking charge over your eating behaviors, and will be gaining control over your energy supply.

TODAY'S MENU
8am: bowl of cereal with fruit
10 am: An energy bar
12 pm: Turkey breast sandwich with vegetable soup
2 pm: Baked potato and cottage cheese
4 pm: An energy bar
5:30: Run/walk
6:15: Finish exercise, glass of Endurox R4
7:30: Family dinner, no dessert
9 pm: Fruit with fat-free vanilla yogurt

Eating every 2 hours may burn off 8-10 pounds a year

As mentioned in the previous chapter, if you have not eaten for about 3 hours, your body senses that it is going into a starvation mode, and slows down the metabolism rate while increasing the production of fat-depositing enzymes. This means you will not be burning as many calories as normal, you won't be as mentally and physically alert and more of your next meal will be stored away as fat.

If the starvation reflex starts working after 3 hours, then eat every 2 hours. This is a great way to burn more calories. A person who now eats 2-3 times a day can burn 8-10 extra pounds a year when she shifts to eating 8-10 times a day. This assumes equal calories are eaten under each meal frequency pattern.

Big meals slow you down

Big meals are a big production for the digestive system. Blood is diverted to the long and winding intestine and the stomach. Because of the workload, the body tends to reduce blood flow to other areas, leaving you feeling more lethargic and sedentary.

Small meals speed you up

Smaller amounts of food can usually be processed quickly without putting a burden on the digestive system. Each time you eat a small meal or snack your metabolism revs up. A metabolism increase several times a day means calories burned—and sustained energy for the next hour or two.

You also give a setback to your set point

When you wait more than three hours between meals, the set point engages the starvation reflex. But if you eat every 2-3 hours, the starvation reflex is often not engaged—due to the regular supply of food.

Motivation increases when you eat more often

Low motivation in the afternoon is often due to not eating regularly enough during the day: not eating breakfast, not eating enough total calories throughout the day, and eating very little from lunch to afternoon workout time. If you have not eaten for 4 hours or more, and you're scheduled for a workout that afternoon, you will often not feel very motivated—because of low blood sugar and low metabolism. You can turn this around, even when you've had a bad eating day, by having a snack 30-60 minutes before exercise. A fibrous energy bar with a cup of coffee (tea, diet drink) can reverse the negative mindset and energy deficit. Eating breakfast and then eating every 2-3 hours can keep your energy flowing.

Satisfaction from a small meal—to avoid overeating

The number of calories you eat per day can be reduced by choosing foods and combinations of foods that leave you satisfied longer. Sugar is the worst problem in calorie control and satisfaction. When you drink a beverage with sugar in it, the sugar will be processed very quickly, and you will often be hungry within 30 minutes— even after consuming a high quantity of calories. This will usually lead to two undesirable outcomes:

1. Eating more food to satisfy hunger

2. Staying hungry and triggering the starvation reflex

Your mission is to find the right combination of foods in your small meals that will leave you satisfied for 2-3 hours. Then, eat another snack that will do the same. You will find a growing number of food combinations that probably have fewer calories, but keep you from getting hungry until your next snack.

Nutrients that leave you satisfied longer:

Fat

A certain amount of fat in a snack or meal will leave you satisfied longer because it slows down digestion, but a little goes a long way. When the fat content of a meal goes beyond 30%, you start to feel more lethargic due to the fact that fat is harder to digest. While up to about 25% of the calories in fat (during a snack or a meal) will help you hold hunger at bay, a lot of fat can compromise a fat-burning program. Fat is automatically deposited on your body. None of the dietary fat is used for energy. When you eat a fatty meal, you might as well inject the fat grams onto your hips or stomach. The fat you burn as fuel must be broken down from the stored fat on your body. So it helps to eat a little fat in a snack but too much of it will mean more fat on your body.

Bad fat: There are two kinds of fat that have been found to cause narrowing of the arteries around the heart and leading to your brain: saturated fat and trans fat. Mono and unsaturated fats, from vegetable sources, are often healthy—olive oil, nuts, avocado, safflower oil. Some fish oils have Omega 3 fatty acids which have been shown to have a protective effect on the heart. Many fish have oil that is not protective—so check this out. Most of the fat in animal products is saturated fat.

Look carefully at the labels because a lot of prepared foods have vegetable oils that have been processed into trans fat. A wide range

of baked goods and other foods have trans fat. It helps to check the labels, and call the 800 number to ask about foods that don't break down the fat composition. Another simple solution is to simply avoid the foods that aren't well-labeled—especially baked goods.

Protein—go for the lean!
You need protein every day for rebuilding the muscle that is broken down during exercise, as well as normal wear and tear. Runners, even those who log high mileage, don't need to eat significantly more protein than sedentary people. But if endurance exercisers don't get their usual amount of protein, they'll feel more aches and pains (and general weakness) sooner than average people.

Having protein with each meal will leave you feeling satisfied for a longer period of time. But eating more protein calories than you need will produce a conversion of the excess into fat. A general guideline for daily intake of protein is one-half a gram for every pound of body weight (or .9 gram of protein for each kilogram of body weight).

Recently, protein has been added to sports drinks with great success. When a drink with 80% carbohydrate and 20% protein (such as Accelerade) is consumed within 30 minutes of the start of exercise, glycogen is activated better, and energy is supplied sooner and better. By consuming a drink that has the same ratio (like Endurox R4) within 30 minutes of the finishing of a workout, the reloading of the muscles has been shown to be more complete.

Complex carbohydrates give you a "discount" and a "grace period". Foods such as celery, beans, cabbage, spinach, turnip greens, grape nuts, whole grain cereal, etc., can burn up to 25% of the calories in digestion. As opposed to fat (which is directly deposited on your body after eating it), only the excess carbs are processed into fat. After dinner, for example, you have the opportunity to burn off any excess that you acquired during the day. The extra fiber in these foods leaves you satisfied longer.

Fat + Protein + Complex Carbs = SATISFACTION
Eating a snack that has a variety of the three satisfaction ingredients above will lengthen the time that you'll feel satisfied—even after small meals. These three items take longer to digest, and therefore keep the metabolism rate revved up.

Other important nutrients...

Fiber
When fiber is put into foods, it slows down digestion and maintains the feeling of satisfaction longer. Soluble fiber, such as oat bran, seems to bestow a longer feeling of satisfaction than unsoluble fiber, such as wheat bran. But any type of fiber will help in this regard.

Recommended percentages of the three nutrients

There are differing opinions on this issue. Here are the ranges given by a number of top nutritionists I have read and interviewed. These are listed in terms in the percentage of the daily total of calories in each nutrient.

Protein: between 15% and 25%
Fat: between 15% and 25%
Carbohydrate: whatever is left—hopefully in
complex carbohydrates.

Simple carbs help us add fat

These are the "feel good" foods: candy, baked sweets, starches like mashed potatoes and rice, sugar drinks (including fruit juice and sports drinks) and most desserts. Some simple carbs are good when consumed within 30 minutes of finishing a strenuous workout. But when you're on a fat-burning mission you need to minimize the amount of these foods.

The sugar in these products is digested so quickly that you get little or no lasting satisfaction from them. They often leave you with a craving for more of them which, if denied, will activate a starvation reflex. Because they are processed quickly, you become hungry relatively quickly and will eat, accumulating extra calories that usually end up as fat at the end of the day.

As mentioned in the last chapter, it is never a good idea to eliminate all of the simple carb foods that you like. The worst situation is to say "I'll never eat another...". This starts the ticking of a starvation-reflex timebomb: at some point in the future, when the food is around and no one else is, you will eat and eat. Keep taking a bite or two of the foods you dearly love when you have cravings—but only a bite or two. At the same time, cultivate an appreciation for the taste of foods with more fiber and little or no refined sugar or fat.

#19

Good Blood Sugar = Motivation

Your blood sugar level (BSL) determines how good you feel. When it is at an adequate, moderate level you feel stable, energized, and motivated. If you eat too much sugar, your BSL can rise too high. You'll feel really good for a while. But the excess sugar triggers a release of insulin, that usually pushes BSL too low. In this state, you don't have energy, mental focus is hazy, and motivation drops.

When BSL is maintained at a stable level throughout the day, you will be more motivated to exercise, and will welcome adding other movement to your life. You'll have a more positive mental attitude, and be more likely to deal with stress, and solve problems. Just as eating throughout the day maintains metabolism, the steady infusion of balanced nutrients all day long will maintain stable blood sugar.

You don't want to get on the "bad side" of your BSL. Low levels are a stress on the system and literally mess with your mind. Your brain is fueled by blood sugar and when the supply goes down, your mental stress goes up. If you have not eaten for several hours before a run, you'll receive an increase in the number of negative messages telling you don't have the energy to exercise, that it will hurt, and many others.

The simple act of eating a snack that has carbohydrate and about 20% protein will reduce the negative, make you feel good, and help to get you out the door. Keeping a snack as a BSL booster can often be the difference whether you work out that day or not.

The BSL roller coaster

Eating a snack with too many calories of simple carbohydrate can be counter-productive for BSL maintenance. As mentioned above, when the BSL gets too high, your body produces insulin, resulting in a a BSL drop. The tendency is to eat again, which produces excess calories that are converted into fat. But if you don't eat, you'll stay hungry and pretty miserable—in no mood to exercise or move around and burn calories.

Eating every 2-3 hours is best

When exercisers experiment with various snacks, most find that an individualized arrangement of small meals produces a level BSL.

As noted in the previous chapter, it's best to combine complex carbs with protein and a small amount of fat to achieve this result.

Do I have to eat before a run? Only if your blood sugar is low
Most who exercise in the morning don't need to eat anything before the start. As mentioned above, if your blood sugar level is low in the afternoon and you have a workout scheduled, a snack can help when it is taken about 30 minutes before. If you feel that a morning snack will help, the only issue is to avoid consuming so much that you get an upset stomach.

For best results in raising blood sugar when it is too low (within 30 minutes before exercise), a snack should have about 80% of the calories in simple carbohydrate and 20% in protein. This promotes the production of insulin which is helpful in getting the glycogen in your muscles, ready for use. The product Accelerade has worked best among the thousands of exercisers I hear from every year. It has the 80%/20% ratio of carb to protein. If you eat an energy bar with the 80/20 ratio, be sure to drink 6-8 oz of water with it.

Eating during exercise
Most exercisers don't need to worry about eating or drinking during a run or walk until the length of the session exceeds 60 minutes. At this point, there are several options. Most will wait until they have been exercising for about 40 minutes before starting to take the first booster snack—but this time will vary with individuals.

Gel products—these come in small packets, and are the consistency of honey or thick syrup. The most successful way to take them is to put 1-2 packets into a small plastic bottle with a pop-top. About every 10-15 minutes, take a squirt or two, with a sip or two of water

Energy bars—cut into 8-10 pieces and take a piece, with a couple of sips of water, every 10-15 minutes.

Candy—particularly gummi bears. The usual consumption is 3-5 small units, about every 10-15 minutes.

Sports Drinks—since there is significant percentage of nausea among those who drink these during exercise, this is not my top recommendation. If you have that a product works for you, use it exactly as you have used it before.

It is important to re-load after exercise—within 30 minutes
Whenever you have finished a hard or long workout (for you), a reloading snack of 100-200 calories will help you recover faster. Again, the 80%/20% ratio of carb to protein has been most successful in reloading the muscles. The product that has worked best among the thousands I work with each year is Endurox R4.

An Exerciser's Diet

A radical change in the foods you are used to eating, is not a good idea, and usually leads to problems. If you want to make dietary changes, do so gradually.

As a regular exerciser you will not need significantly more vitamins and minerals, protein, etc. than a sedentary person. But if you don't get these ingredients for several days in a row, you will feel the effects when you try to exercise.

Most important nutrient: water

Whether you take in your fluids as water, juice or other fluids, you should drink regularly throughout the day. Under normal circumstances, your thirst is a good guide for fluid consumption, but this is not the case among runners over @ 45—when the thirst mechanism breaks down. The equivalent of 6-8 glasses of various fluids is a good guide, but if you are sweating a great deal, you will need to consume more. Alcoholic drinks are dehydrating. The fluid in caffeine beverages is only worth about half the fluid from water.

If you have to take bathroom stops during walks or runs, you are usually drinking too much—either before or during the exercise. During an exercise session of 60 minutes or less, most exercisers don't need to drink at all. The intake of fluid before exercise should be arranged so that the excess fluid is eliminated before the start. Each person is a bit different, so you will have to find a routine that works for you. Very few individuals have to take potty breaks when they don't drink within 2 hours before the start of a workout or race.

Hyponatremia—dangerous consumption of too much water

If you're running more than 4 hours and are drinking more than 27 oz of fluid, you could be producing a dangerous depletion of sodium that could lead to death. Women are much more prone to this condition than men, possibly because they tend to drink more fluid for their body weight than men. Symptoms of this condition include the following, but none may be present:

- swelling of hands (to twice normal size)
- cramping in legs
- significant loss of concentration
- diarrhea or vomiting—if exercising for more than 4 hours and suffering from either, get help immediately

Here's how to prevent this dangerous condition.

- Drink no more than 27 oz of fluid an hour
- Avoid taking anti-inflammatory medication before or during a run of more than 4 hours
- Talk to your doctor about any medication you are taking— mentioning hyponatremia and that you plan to run more than 4 hours. Follow the doctor's advice concerning medication issues
- If you cramp regularly, ask your doctor if you can take a salt tablet during exercise (SUCCEED is a good one).

Sweat the electrolytes

Electrolytes are the salts that your body loses when you sweat: sodium (primary), potassium (secondary but needed), magnesium and calcium (trace amounts needed each day). When these minerals get too low, your fluid transfer system doesn't work as well and you may experience ineffective cooling, swelling of the hands, and other problems. Most exercisers have no problem replacing these in a normal diet. But if you are experiencing cramping during or after exercise, regularly, you may be low in sodium or potassium. The best product I've found for replacing these minerals is called SUCCEED. If you have high blood pressure, get your doctor's guidance before taking any salt supplement.

Practical eating issues

- You don't need to eat before exercise, unless your blood sugar is low (see the previous chapter)

- Reload most effectively by eating within 30 minutes of the finish of a run/walk (80% carb/20% protein)

- Eating or drinking too much right before the start can interfere with deep breathing, & may cause side pain. The food or fluid in your stomach, limits your intake of air into the lower lungs, and restricts the diaphragm.

- If you are running low on blood sugar at the end of your long workouts, take some blood sugar booster with you (see the previous chapter for suggestions)

- It is never a good idea to eat a huge meal. Those who claim that they must "carbo load" are usually rationalizing the desire to eat a lot of food. Eating a big meal the night before (or the day of) a long workout can be a real problem. You will have a lot of food in your gut, and you will be bouncing up and down for an extended period. Get the picture?

When you are sweating a lot, it is a good idea to drink several glasses a day of a good electrolyte beverage. Accelerade, by Pacific Health Labs, is the best I've seen for both maintaining fluid levels and electrolyte levels.

Vitamins and minerals

We strongly recommend a vitamin supplement, as a nutritional insurance policy. The best product we've found, based upon the research, is Cooper Complete. This high quality product is produced by Dr. Kenneth Cooper from Dallas, Texas. There are several products for women at various stages of life. For more information, visit *www.coopercomplete.com.*

Calcium

The amount of calcium suggested for women who are approaching or experiencing menopause is 1500 mg per day. For most other women, the recommendation is 1000 mg a day. Be sure to read the section on women's issues about osteoporosis.

Iron

Pre-menopausal women tend to be low in iron. Exercise pushes the level even lower because the more you sweat, the more iron you lose. Cooking food in an iron skillet is an excellent way of getting iron that can be easily assimilated. Iron supplements are often hard to assimilate, so check with your doctor if you are low in this nutrient. The best test is the serum ferritin test. Standard blood iron tests are not as effective in identifying low levels for exercisers. Post menopausal women do not tend to have as many low iron issues. Each person should monitor this through your regular physicals/blood work.

What about caffeine

Research has shown that the consumption of the equivalent of a cup of coffee will extend endurance, and increase the fat burning potential. This central nervous system booster can rev up the muscles and get your performance systems working to capacity. Unless you have heart rhythm problems, caffeine sensitivities, or other related problems, caffeine may enhance the way you feel and the effort level, during exercise.

Meal ideas

Morning options

- Whole-grain bread made into french toast with fruit yogurt, juice, or frozen juice concentrate as syrup
- Whole-grain pancakes with fruit and yogurt
- A bowl of Grape Nuts Cereal, skim milk, non-fat yogurt, and fruit
- Non-fat cottage cheese with fruit

Lunch/afternoon options

- Tuna fish sandwich, whole grain bread, a little low-fat mayo, cole slaw (with low-fat dressing)
- Turkey breast sandwich with salad, low-fat cheese, celery & carrots
- Veggie burger on whole-grain bread, low-fat mayo, salad of choice
- Spinach salad with dried cranberries, a few peanuts, or sunflower seeds, or almonds, or low-fat cheese, non-fat dressing, whole grain rolls or croutons

Evening options

There are lots of great recipes in publications such as COOKING LIGHT. The basics are listed below. What makes the meal come alive are the seasonings which are listed in the recipes. You can use a variety of fat substitutes.

- Fish or lean chicken breast or tofu (or other protein source) with whole-wheat pasta, and steamed vegetables
- Rice with vegetables, and a protein source
- Dinner salad with lots of different vegetables, nuts, lean cheese or turkey, or fish, or chicken

Nutrition Advice from Nancy Clark

Note: Nancy is one of the foremost experts in nutrition for exercise

Myth: You must exercise in order to lose body fat

To lose body fat, you must create a calorie deficit. You can create that deficit by adding exercise (which improves your overall health and fitness) or by eating fewer calories. Sick people commonly lose body fat but they do not exercise; they create a calorie deficit. Similarly, injured athletes can also lose fat despite lack of exercise. But the more common story is the following. "I gained weight when I was injured because I couldn't exercise" could more correctly be stated "I gained weight when I was injured because I was bored and depressed. I overate for comfort and entertainment..."

Myth: The more you exercise, the more fat you lose

Often, the more you exercise, the hungrier you get and—
- the more you eat, or
– the more your believe you "deserve" to eat, or
-the more you want to eat as a reward for having both gotten to the gym and survived the exercise session.

But if you spend 60 minutes in a spin class and burn off 600 calories, only to reward yourself with 12 Oreos (600 calories), you quickly wipe out your weight loss efforts in less than 3 minutes...

The effects of exercise on weight loss are complex and unclear. We know among older people (56-78 years) who participated in a vigorous walking program, daily calorie needs remained about the same (2,400 without exercise, 2,480 with exercise). How could that be? Well, the participants napped more and were 62% less active throughout the rest of their day. (1)

Another study with post-menopausal women found the same results from 8 weeks of moderate exercise training. Their 24-hour energy expenditure remained similar from the start to the end of the program. (2) The bottom line: You have to eat according to your whole day's activity level, not according to how hard you trained that day.

Myth: If you train for a marathon, your body fat will melt away

Wishful thinking. I commonly hear marathoners, triathletes and other highly competitive endurance athletes complain "For all the exercise I do, I should be pencil thin..." They fail to lose fat because, like the fitness exercisers described above, they put all of their energy into exercising, but then tend to be quite sedentary the rest of the day as they recover from their tough workouts. A study with male endurance athletes who reported a seemingly low calorie intake found they did less spontaneous activity than their peers in the non-exercise parts of their day. (3) The bottom line: you need to keep taking the stairs instead of the elevators, no matter how much you train!

Alternatively, athletes who complain they eat like a bird but fail to lose body fat may simply be under-reporting their food intake. A survey of female marathoners indicated the fatter runners under-report their food intake more so than their leaner peers. (4) Remember: calories mindlessly eaten standing up or on-the-run count just as much as calories from meals.

Myth: Couples who exercise together, lose fat together

In a 16-month study looking at exercise for weight loss, men and women completed an identical amount of exercise. The men lost 11.5 pounds; the women maintained weight! (5) In another study with previously sedentary, normal weight men and women who participated in an 18-month marathon training program, the men increased their calorie intake by about 500 per day; the women increased by only 60 calories—despite having added on 50 miles per week of running. The men lost about five pounds of fat; the women two pounds. (6)

What's going on here??? Well, a husband who adds on exercise is likely to lose more weight than his wife because he's likely heftier and thereby burns more calories during the same workout. But, speaking in terms of evolution, Nature seems protective of women's role as childbearer, and wants women to maintain adequate body fat for nourishing healthy babies. Hence, women are more energy efficient. Obesity researchers at NY's Columbia University suggest a pound of weight loss in men equates to a deficit of about 2,500 calories, while women need a 3,500 calorie deficit!!! (7) No wonder women have a tougher time losing weight than men....

The bottom line

If you are exercising to lose weight, I encourage you to separate exercise and weight. Yes, you should exercise for health, fitness, stress relief and, most importantly, for enjoyment. (After all, the E in exercise stands for enjoyment!) I discourage you from exercising to burn off calories; that makes exercise feels like punishment for having excess body fat. When exercise is something you do to your body, rather than do for your body, you'll eventually quit exercising. Bad idea. Pay attention to your calorie intake. Knocking off just 100 calories a day from your evening snacks can theoretically result in 10 pounds a year of fat loss. Seems simpler than hours of sweating...?

References:
1. Goran, *Am J Physiol* 263:E950, 1992
2. Keytel, *Int J Sport Nutr* 11:226, 2001
3. Thompson, *Med Sci Sports Exerc* 27::347, 1995
4. Edwards, *Med Sci Sports Exer* 25:1398, 1993
5. Donnelly, *Arch Intern Med* 163:1343, 2003
6. Janssen, *Int J Sports Med,* 10:S1,1989
7. Pietrobelli *Int J Obes Relat Metab Disord* 26:1339, 2002

Taming the cookie monster

"I know I shouldn't eat cookies–but I just can't help myself. I'm a cookie monster!"

Sound familiar? Everyone knows that cookies (and candy, cakes, pies, ice cream, other sweets) offer suboptimal nutrition. But why are cookies so popular? Why do we eat monstrous portions that were not a part of our food intentions?

Why? Because cookies (and other sweets) taste good. Because athletes–and all people, for that matter–who get too hungry tend to crave sweets. Most athletes believe cookies are the problem. I challenge that belief. I see cookies as being the symptom and getting too hungry as being the problem. That is, when you get too hungry, you experience a very strong drive to eat. Cookies!!!

Hunger, a simple request for fuel. Hunger is a very powerful physiological force that creates a strong desire to eat. When a child complains about being hungry, the parent readily provides food. But when athletes experience hunger, they either have "no time" to eat or, if weight-conscious, they fear food as being fattening; eating equates to getting fat. Most athletes eat without getting fat. Food, after all, is fuel. But cookie monster problems arise when time-deprived or dieting athletes consume inadequate fuel and hunger becomes the norm. The result is an abnormal physiological state known as starvation –or more commonly, known as being "on a diet." Although starvation is associated with famine in poor countries, starvation is also common among busy and dieting athletes.

In 1950, Ancel Keys and his colleagues at the University of Minnesota studied the physiology of starvation. They carefully monitored 36 young, healthy, psychologically normal men who for 6 months were allowed to eat only half their normal intake (similar to a very restrictive reducing diet). For 3 months prior to this semi-starvation diet, the researchers carefully studied each man's behaviors, personality, and eating patterns. They also observed the men for three to nine months of refeeding.

As the subjects' body weight fell, the researchers learned that many of the symptoms that might have been thought to be specific to binge eating were actually the result of starvation. The most striking change was a dramatic increase with food preoccupation. The hungry subjects thought about food all the time. They talked about it, read about it, dreamed about it, even collected recipes. They dramatically increased their consumption of coffee and tea, and chewed gum excessively. They became depressed, had severe mood swings, experienced irritability, anger and anxiety. They became withdrawn and lost their sense of humor.

They had cold hands and feet, and felt weak and dizzy. During the study, some of the men were unable to maintain control over food; they would binge eat if the opportunity presented itself—similar to "breaking a diet" or bingeing on cookies. When the study ended and the men could eat freely, many of them ate continuously—big meals followed by snacks. They ate and ate—like a cookie monster. So what can we learn about binge-eating from this study?

1. Preoccupation with cookies (and sweets) indicates your body is too hungry. Hunger creates a strong physiological drive to eat.
2. Cookie binges stem from starvation. If you are unable to stop eating once you start, you have likely gotten monstrously hungry (or are very stressed).
3. Dieters who restrict to the point of semi-starvation are likely to "blow their diets" and consequently acquire some benefits: less hunger, cookies (and other sweets), and more energy.

Living without hunger

In our society, people live in hunger because the prevailing messages are "I don't have time to eat" and "food is fattening." Athletes believe the best way to lose weight is to severely restrict calories. The only opportunity dieters have to eat cookies (and other tasty foods) is when they "blow" their diets and turn into cookie monsters. But there is another way to manage cookies: 1) prevent hunger by eating enough at meals. You can lose weight by eating 10% to 20% fewer calories, not 50% fewer. 2) enjoy a cookie or two as a part of an overall healthful daily food plan. To know how many calories (and cookies) you are entitled to eat to negate hunger and manage your weight, do this simple math:

- Take your weight (or a good weight for your body) and multiply it by 10. This estimates your resting metabolic rate (RMR, the amount of energy you need to simply exist, pump blood, breathe, etc.). If you weigh 140 pounds, your RMR is about 1,400 calories—the amount you'd burn if you were to run for 14 miles!

- Add to your RMR about half that number for activities of daily living. For example, if you weigh 140 pounds and are moderately active (without your purposeful exercise), you need about 700 calories for daily living. Add fewer calories if you are sedentary.

- Next, add calories for purposeful exercise. For example, a 140-lb person would need about 1,400 calories (RMR) + 700 (daily living) + 300 (for 30 minutes of exercise) = 2,400 calories to maintain weight. To lose weight, deduct 20%, to about 1,900 calories. This translates into 600 calories for breakfast/snack, 700 for lunch/snack, and 600 for dinner/snack (or the equivalent of 11-13 Fig Newtons per section of the day.)

The next time you get into a cookie frenzy, use food labels to calculate your day's intake. You'll likely see a huge discrepancy between what you have eaten and what your body deserves. No wonder you are craving cookies! Once you recognize the power of hunger, you can take steps to prevent it by eating before you get too hungry.

Living with cookies

If you like cookies too much—to the extent you have trouble stopping eating them once you start—the way to take the power away from cookies is to eat them more often (in appropriate portions) and not try to "stay away from them." Apples likely have no "power" over you because you give yourself permission to eat an apple whenever you want. But cookies will have power over you if you routinely restrict them. By enjoying a cookie with every lunch, you'll start to want fewer cookies. They will lose their appeal and the cookie monster will rest in its cage, peacefully.

Nancy Clark, MS, RD counsels sports-active people at Healthworks (617-383-6100) in Chestnut Hill, MA. Her Sports Nutrition Guidebook, Third Edition ($23) and her Food Guide for Marathoners, Second Edition 2007 ($16,95) has more information on weight control. These are available at www.nancyclarkrd.com or www.JeffGalloway.com.

#22

Running Form

You are probably running the right way! Studies show that the human organism finds the most efficient way to run. Research indicates that almost all runners are at their best efficiency or very close to it. In other words, there is no "correct" way to run or walk, except the way that is natural for you. If you're moving forward without pain, you have good form.

The suggestions in this chapter are only offered to help you avoid "form induced" aches and pains. The human body has a wonderful way of adapting to our body structure and individual differences. Your right brain (the intuitive part) is searching for easier ways of moving forward and making small adaptations if you regularly exercise. If you're not having aches and pains, don't make changes in your form. But when in doubt—adjust form so that it is easier, with less exertion, and no aches.

Running is an inertial activity. The first few strides get the body in motion, and from that point your mission is just to keep the momentum, using minimal energy. Very little strength is needed to run, and it has already been developed. Just flow with your forward motion.

Humans have many bio-mechanical adaptations working for them, which have been made more efficient over more than a million years of walking and running. The mechanical origin of movement efficiency in humans is the combination of the ankle and the Achilles tendon. This is an extremely sophisticated system of levers, springs, balancing devices, and more—involving hundreds of component parts which are amazingly well coordinated. Bio-mechanics experts believe that this degree of development was not needed for walking. When our ancient ancestors had to run to survive, the evolution reached a new level of performance.

With the right balance of walking and running, a very little amount of effort from the calf muscle produces a smooth continuation of forward movement. As this muscle gets in better shape, and improves endurance, you can keep going, mile after mile, with little perceived effort. Other muscle groups offer support and fine-tune the process. When you feel aches and pains that might be due to the way you run, going back to the minimal use of the ankle and Achilles tendon can often leave you feeling smooth and efficient very quickly.

A better way of running?

There may be a better way to run for you, a pattern of motion that will leave your legs with more strength and fewer aches and pains after every workout. Repeated research on runners, however, has shown that most are very close to their ideal efficiency. I believe this is due to the action of the right brain. After tens of thousands of steps, it keeps searching for (and finding) the most efficient pattern of motion for feet, legs, and body.

In my running schools, and weekend retreats I conduct an individual running form analysis for each runner. After having analyzed over 10 thousand runners, I've also found that most are running in a very efficient way. The problems are seldom big ones—but usually a series of small mistakes. By making a few minor adjustments, most runners can feel better on every run.

The big three: posture, stride, and bounce

In these consultations, I've also discovered that when runners have problems, they tend to occur in three areas: Posture, stride, and bounce. And the problems tend to be specific to the individual, occurring in specific areas. Fatigue brings on most of the problems relating to form. A slight overstride (even a fraction of an inch), can increase tightness and muscle weakness at the end of a run. As a tired body "wobbles", other muscle groups try to keep the body on course, but are not designed for this, and can be pushed into soreness or injury.

If you feel relaxed and running is easy even at the end of a run—you're probably running correctly

Overall, the running motion should feel easy. There should be no tension in your neck, back, shoulders or legs. A good way to correct problems is to change posture, foot or leg placement, etc., so that running is easier and there is no tightness or pain.

Posture

Good running posture is actually good body posture. The head is naturally balanced over the shoulders, which are aligned over the hips. As the foot comes underneath, all of these elements are in balance so that no energy is needed to prop up the body. You shouldn't have to work to pull a wayward body back from a wobble or inefficient motion.

Forward lean can lead to back or neck pain

The posture errors tend to be mostly due to a forward lean—especially when we are tired. The head wants to get to the finish as soon as possible, but the legs can't go any faster. In their first races, beginners are often the ones whose heads are literally ahead of the body, which produces more than a few falls around the finish line. A forward lean will often concentrate fatigue, soreness and tightness in the lower back or neck.

It all starts with the head. When the neck muscles are relaxed, the head is usually in a natural position. If there is tension in the neck, or soreness afterward, the head is usually leaning too far forward. This triggers a more general upper body imbalance in which the head and chest are suspended slightly ahead of the hips and feet. If you have neck or back pain or fatigue, ask a running companion to tell you if and when your head is too far forward, or leaning down. The ideal position of the head is mostly upright, with your eyes focused about 30-40 yards ahead of you.

Sitting back can lead to sore hips
The hips are the other major postural component that can shift out of alignment. A runner with this problem, when observed from the side, will have the butt behind the rest of the body. When the pelvis area is shifted back, the legs are not allowed to go through a natural range of motion, and the stride length becomes short. This produces a slower pace, even when spending significant effort. Many runners tend to hit harder on their heels when their hips are shifted back. The most common symptom is sore hips after a run.

A backward lean is rare
It is rare for runners to lean back, but it happens. In my experience, this is usually due to a structural problem in the spine or hips. If you do this, and you're having pain in the neck, back or hips, you should see an orthopedist who knows a bit about running biomechanics.

Correction: "Puppet on a string"
The best correction I've found to postural problems has been this mental exercise: imagine that you are a puppet on a string.

Suspended from up above like a puppet—from the head and each side of the shoulders—your head lines up above the shoulders, the hips come directly underneath, and the feet naturally touch lightly. It won't hurt anyone to do the "puppet" several times during a run.

It helps to combine this image with a deep breath. About every 4-5 minutes, as you start to run after a walk break, take a deep, lower lung breath, straighten up and say "I'm a puppet". Then imagine that you don't have to spend energy maintaining this upright posture, because the strings attached from above keep you on track. As you continue to do this, you reinforce good posture, and set your intuitive powers on making this behavior a habit.

An oxygen dividend

Breathing improves when you straighten up. A leaning body can't get ideal use out of the lower lungs. This can cause side pain. When you run upright the lower lungs can receive adequate air and absorb oxygen better.

Feet low to the ground

The most efficient stride is a shuffle—with feet next to the ground. As long as you pick your foot up enough to avoid stumbling over a rock or uneven pavement, stay low to the ground. Most runners don't need more than 1" clearance.

Your ankle and Achilles tendon form a mechanical unit that will act as a spring, moving you forward with very little effort required.

Through this "shuffling" technique, running becomes almost automatic. When runners err on bounce, they try to push off too hard. This usually results in extra effort spent in lifting the body off the ground. You can think of this as energy wasted in the air— energy that could be used to run another mile or two.

The correction for too much bounce: Light touch drill

The ideal foot touch should be so light that you don't feel yourself pushing off or landing. This means that your foot stays low to the ground and goes though an efficient and natural motion. During the middle of a run, time yourself for 20 seconds. Focus on one item: touching so softly that you don't hear your feet. Earplugs are not allowed for this drill. Imagine that you are running on thin ice or through a bed of hot coals. Do several of these 20 second touches, becoming quieter and quieter.

Stride length

Studies have shown that as runners get faster, the stride length shortens. This clearly shows that the key to faster and more efficient running is increased cadence or turnover of feet and legs. A major cause of aches, pains and injuries is a stride length that is too long. When in doubt, it is always better to err on the side of having a shorter stride.

Don't lift your knees!

Sore thighs are often caused by a high knee lift, which often happens at the end of a tiring run. This can also extend the stride outside your mechanical efficiency.

Don't kick out too far in front of you!

Tightness in the front of the shin, or behind the knee, or in the hamstring (back of the thigh) is a sign that you are kicking too far forward, and reaching out too far. Correct this by staying low to the ground, shortening the stride, and lightly touching the ground— more of a shuffle.

Cadence or turnover drill—improves efficiency

This easy drill, done once a week, brings together all of the elements of good running form.

1. Warm up by walking for 5 minutes, and running and walking very gently for 10 minutes.
2. Start jogging slowly for 1-2 minutes, and then time yourself for 30 seconds. During this half minute, count the number of times your left foot touches.
3. Walk around for a minute or so.
4. On the second 30 second drill, increase the count by 1.
5. Repeat this 3-7 more times. Each time trying to increase by 1 additional count.

In the process of improving turnover, the body's internal monitoring system coordinates a series of adaptations which pulls together all of the form components into an efficient team:

- Your foot touches more gently
- Extra, inefficient motions of the foot and leg are reduced or eliminated
- Less effort is spent on pushing up or pushing forward
- You stay lower to the ground
- The ankle becomes more efficient
- Ache and pain areas are not overused

 # 23

Staying Injury Free

Because running and walking enabled our ancient ancestors to survive, our bodies are designed to adapt to the running motion without pain, when done according to the following:

- Run at a gentle pace—and insert walk breaks from the beginning
- Rest sufficiently after each workout
- Exercise regularly but not too often—about every other day
- Increase gradually, and reduce the intensity of the longer workout
- The single greatest reason for running improvement is not getting injured

Be sensitive to weak links

Each of us has a very few areas that accumulate more stress because of the way we run, posture, etc. These are usually the sites of most of our injuries. The most common body parts are the knees, the foot, the shins, and the hip. If you have a particular place on your knee that has been injured before, and it hurts during or after exercise, take an extra day or two off, and follow the suggestions concerning treating an injury, listed below.

How do you know that you are injured?

The following are the leading signs that you have an injury. If you experience any of the three below, you should stop your workout immediately and take some extra rest days (usually 2-3). Even when you continue to run for another 5 minutes when injured, you can dramatically increase the damage, requiring 3 weeks or 3 months—instead of 3 days.

1. *Inflammation*—any type of swelling
2. *Loss of function*—the knee, foot, etc., doesn't work correctly
3. *Pain*—that does not go away when you walk for a few minutes

Losing conditioning

Studies have shown that you can maintain conditioning even when you don't exercise for 5 days. In most cases runners only need to stop for 2-3 days.

Treatment

It is always best, at the first sign of a real injury, to see a doctor (or with muscle injury—a massage therapist) who wants to get you exercising again as soon as possible. The better doctors will explain what they believe is wrong (or tell you that he/she cannot come up with a diagnosis) and give you a treatment plan. This will give you great confidence in the process, which has been shown to speed the healing. A podiatrist specializes in the foot, or in problems that result from a condition in the foot. An orthopedist is trained to deal with most injuries that result from running. Sometimes orthopedists specialize in a specific part of the body.

Treatments while you are waiting to see a doctor

Unfortunately, most of the better doctors are so booked up that it may take several days and sometime weeks to see them. While waiting for your appointment, here are some things other runners/walkers have done when one of the weak links kick in:

1. Take at least 2-5 days off from any activity that could irritate it.
2. If you must stop running for more than 5 days, do some walking or water running to maintain your conditioning—if these activities don't irritate the injury.
3. If the area is next to the skin (tendon, foot, etc.), rub a chunk of ice on the area(s)—constantly rubbing for 15 minutes until the area gets numb. Continue to do this for a week after you feel no symptoms. The chunk of ice must be rubbed constantly and directly on the tissue where the injury is located.
4. If the problem is inside a joint or muscle, call your doctor and ask if you can use prescription strength anti-inflammatory medication. Don't take any medication without a doctor's advice—and follow that advice.
5. If you have a muscle injury, see a very successful sports massage therapist. Try to find one who has a lot of successful experience treating the area where you are injured. The magic fingers and hands can often work wonders.

Preventing injury

Having had over a hundred injuries myself, and then having worked with tens of thousands who have worked through aches and pains, I offer the suggestions below. They are based upon my experience and are offered as one exerciser to another. I'm proud to report that since I started following the advice that I give others, I've not had an overuse injury in almost 30 years. For all medical issues, see a doctor.

1. Take 48 hours between runs or strenuous walks

Running longer or faster puts a lot more stress on the muscles, tendons, etc. Allowing tired muscles to rest for two days can work like magic in recovery. Stair machine work should also be avoided during the 48-hour rest period (stair work uses the same muscles as running). Also avoid any other activities that seem to irritate the aggravated area.

Don't stretch!

I've come full circle on this. A high percentage of the exercisers who report to me, injured, have either become injured because they stretched or aggravated the injury by stretching. When they stop stretching, most have reported that the injury starts healing in a relatively short period of time. The exception to this rule is in the treatment of ilio-tibial band injury. For this injury alone, stretching the I-T band seems to help runners continue to run while they heal.

Do the "toe squincher" exercise to prevent plantar fasciia

This exercise can be done 10-30 times a day, on both feet (one at a time). Point the toes and contract the muscles in the foot, until the foot cramps (only a few seconds). This strengthens the many little muscles in the foot that can provide a platform of support.

Don't increase total mileage more than 10% a week

Monitor your mileage in a log book or calendar. If you exceed a 10 percent increase, take an extra day off.

Drop total mileage in half, every 3rd or 4th week—even when increasing by no more than 10% per week.

Your log book can guide you here also. You won't lose any conditioning and you'll help the body heal itself, and get stronger. A steady increase, week after week, does not allow the legs to catch up and rebuild.

Avoid a long stride—both walking and running

Use more of a shuffle motion (feet close to the ground), and you'll reduce the chance of many injuries. Even walking with a long stride can irritate the shin muscles. Read the "running form" section for more information in this area.

Your First Race

Neighborhood road races (often for charities) are held almost every weekend, and help runners stay motivated. The participants are not professional athletes. They are busy folks like yourself who are trying to balance exercise, family and work. Neighborhood events not only raise funds for worthy causes, they often create a festival atmosphere where family members, co-workers and you can enjoy exercise. Enrolling in a race is a commitment to yourself to do the training each week to prepare. Finishing is an uplifting reward experience. In more and more of these events, more than half of the participants are women. Almost everyone there is in a good mood.

WHY ENTER A RUNNING EVENT?

- Commitment to a friend or family member: More and more women are training with a neighbor, sister, daughter, etc. Some friends will train in different cities and do the event together as part of a fun weekend.
- Charity: Most events benefit a charity. THE NATIONAL MARATHON TO FIGHT BREAST CANCER, for example, provides an incentive to get in shape, while contributing to an important cause (held at the Mayo clinic in Jacksonville FL, www.breastcancermarathon.com).
- Provide an example to your children: Women who train for and enter events, tend to have more active kids—who become active adults.

What to look for in a race

- Fun and festive—held in an interesting area, part of a town festival, music, expo with exhibits
- Well organized—the organizers... keep things organized: no long lines, easy to register, start goes off on time, water on the course, refreshments for all—even the slowest, no major problems
- Refreshments—some races have water, others have a buffet
- A good T-shirt or other reward—you'll wear it with pride
- The organizers focus on average or beginning runners
- The finish line is kept open for the amount of time you expect to run

Where to find out about races

- Running stores
- Friends who participate
- Running clubs or walking clubs—RRCA, and ARA are two national running organizations Newspaper listings—look at the weekend events listing—often in the lifestyle section.
- Web Searches
- Just do a web search for "road races (your town)" or "5K (your town)". Also try www.signmeup.com, www.active.com and www.marathonguide.com

How to register

1. Online. More and more of the road running/walking events are conducting registration online.
2. When using an entry form, fill out an entry and send it in. You will need to fill out your name, address, T-shirt size, etc, and then sign the waiver form. Be sure to include a entry fee check.
3. Show up on race day. Because some races don't do race day registration, be sure that you can do this. There is usually a penalty for waiting until the last minute—but you can see what the weather is like before you make the trek to the race.

Most common race distance is a 5K (3.1 miles)

This is an excellent distance for your first race, because it's about the shortest distance, and in most areas you will have many from which to choose. Choose a race far enough in the future so that you can increase your endurance through a series of long runs/walks. Your last long one (that is 1-2 miles longer than the distance you plan to run in the race) should be run about 7-10 days before the race itself.

Do the scheduled training for the event—to finish

Use the schedule in this book, or from many of the other good sourcebooks. I strongly suggest that you not try for a time goal on your first one—or pick a time that you know will be easy. Remember that you need to slow down for heat: 30 seconds a mile slower for every 5 degrees above 60°F (20 seconds per kilometer slower for every 2°C above 14°C).

There are successful training schedules for 5K, 10K, and half-marathon in my books: WALKING, GALLOWAY'S BOOK ON RUNNING, A YEAR ROUND PLAN, HALF MARATHON, MARATHON, TESTING YOURSELF. See my www.JeffGalloway.com for more information on these books.

Rehearsal

If at all possible, run one or more of your long ones on the race course. You'll learn how to get there, where to park (or which rapid transit station to exit), and what the site is like. If you will be driving, drive into the parking area several times to make sure you understand how to go exactly where you need to park. This will help you to feel at home with the staging area on race day. Go over the last half-mile of the course at least twice. This is the most important part of the course to know. It's also beneficial to run or walk the first part of the course to see which side of the road is best for walk breaks.

Visualize your line up position: at the back, along the side of the road. If you line up too far forward you could slow down runners that are faster. You want to do this first race slowly, and have a good experience. This is most likely when you start at the back of the pack. Because you will be taking your walk breaks in the race, as you have in training, stay at the side of the road. If there is sidewalk, you can use this for your breaks.

The afternoon before

Don't exercise the day before the race. You won't lose any conditioning if you take two days off. If the race has an expo or other festivities, you may want to attend. Expos feature companies in the running business who display and sell shoes, clothing, books, etc.—often at sale prices. Beware of sale shoes, however. It is best to go to a good running store and go through the procedure noted in the shoe chapter above to select a shoe that is designed for the type of foot you have.

Some races require you to pick up your race number, and sometimes your computer chip (explained below) the day before. Look at the website or the entry form for instructions about this. Most races allow you to pick up your materials on race day. Check on this to be sure.

Race number

This is sometimes called a "bib number". It should be pinned on the front of the garment you'll be wearing when you cross the finish line.

Computer chip

More and more races are using technology that automatically picks up your race number and time as you cross the finish. You must wear this plastic disk that is usually laced on the shoes, near the top. Some races have a velcro band that is attached to the ankle or arm. Read the instructions to make sure you are attaching this correctly. Be sure to turn in the device after the race. The officials have volunteers to collect them, so stop and take them off your shoe, etc. There is a steep fine for those who don't turn in the chip.

The carbo loading dinner

Some races have a dinner the night before. At the dinner you will usually chat with participants at your table, and enjoy the evening.

Don't eat much, however. Many exercisers assume, mistakenly, that they must eat a lot of food the night before. This is actually counterproductive. It takes more than 36 hours for most of the food you eat to be processed and useable in a race—usually longer. There is nothing you can eat the evening before a race that will help you.

But eating too much, or the wrong foods for you, can be a real problem. A lot of food in your gut when you are bouncing up and down in a race is stressful. A very common and embarrassing situation occurs when the gut is emptied to relieve this stress. While you don't want to starve yourself the afternoon and evening before, the best strategy is to eat small meals, and taper down the amount as you get closer to bedtime. As always, it's best to have done a "rehearsal" of eating, so that you know what works, how much, when to stop eating, and what foods to avoid. The day before and the evening before your long run is a good time to work on your eating plan, and replicate the successful routine leading up to raceday.

Drinking

The day before your race, drink about 6 oz of water every 2 hours. As a "hydration insurance policy", drink 6 oz of a good sports drink like Accelerade, 4-6 times throughout the day. Don't drink a lot of fluid during the morning of the race itself. This can lead to bathroom breaks during the race itself. Many races have porto-johns around the course, but some do not. It is a very common practice for participants that have consumed too much fluid that morning to find a tree or alley along the course. To avoid this, stop your fluid intake an hour and a half to two hours before the race so that the fluid is out of the system before the start. Try this before your long runs to find the pattern that works for you.

The night before

Eating is optional after 6pm. If you are hungry, have a very light snack that you have tested before, and has not caused problems. In this situation, I eat about one-fourth of an energy bar. Less is better, but don't go to bed extremely hungry. Eat foods that you know will digest easily—ones that you've eaten successfully the evening before long ones. Continue to have about 8 oz of a good electrolyte beverage like Accelerade over 2 hours before you go to bed.

Alcohol is not recommended the night before, because of the dehydration and central nervous system depressant effects. These usually carry over to the next morning. Some exercisers have no trouble having one glass of wine or beer, while others are better off with none.

Pack your bag and check the contents so that you don't have to think very much on race morning.

- Your watch, set up for the run-walk ratio you are using
- Shoes
- Socks
- Shorts
- Top—see clothing thermometer in the back of this book
- Pin race # on the front of the garment in which you will be finishing
- A few extra safety pins
- Water, Accelerade, pre-race and post race beverages (such as Endurox R4), and a cooler if you wish
- Food for the drive in, and the drive home
- Bandages, Vaseline, any other first aid items you may need
- Cash for registration if you are doing race day registration (check for exact amount, including late fee)
- $25-40 for gas, food, parking, etc.
- Race chip attached according to the race instructions
- A few jokes or stories to provide laughs or entertainment before the start
- A copy of the "race day checklist", which is just below this section
- Prepare your pre/post race drinks (if you have used them in long ones) and put in the refrigerator
- Get the cooler ready to transport any cool drinks you usually use on the way to/from the race

Sleep

You may sleep well, or you may not. Don't worry if you don't sleep at all. Many walkers and runners I work with every year don't sleep at all the night before and have the best race of their lives. Of course, don't try to go sleepless….but if it happens, it is not usually a problem.

Race day checklist

Photocopy this list so that you will not only have a plan, you can carry it out in a methodical way. Pack the list in your race bag. Don't try anything new the day of your race—except for health or safety. The only item I have heard about when used for the first time in a race that has helped, is walk breaks. Even first time users benefit significantly. Otherwise, stick with your plan.

Fluid and potty stops—after you wake up, drink 4-6 oz of water every half hour. If you have used Accelerade about 30 minutes before your long ones, prepare it the night before. Use a cooler if you wish. In order to avoid the bathroom stops, stop your fluid intake according to what has worked for you before.

Eat—but only what you have had success eating before your more difficult runs. It is OK not to eat at all before a race unless you are a diabetic, then go with the plan that you and your doctor have worked out.

Get there early and get your bearings—walk around the site to find where you want to line up (at the back of the pack), and how you will get to the start. Choose a side of the road that has more shoulder or sidewalk for ease in taking walk breaks.

Register or pick up your race number—if you already have all of your materials, you can bypass this step. If not, look at the signage in the registration area and get in the right line. Usually there is one for "race day registration" and one for those who registered online or in the mail and need to pick up their numbers.

Start your warmup @30 minutes before the start. If possible, go backwards on the course for about .5-.6 miles and turn around. This will give you a preview of the most important part of your race—the finish. Here is the warmup routine:

- Walk for 5 minutes, slowly
- Walk and jog in short intervals of 30-60 seconds each for 10 minutes
- Start your watch for the ratio of running and walking (or walking) that you are using and do this for 10 minutes—but at a slower pace than you usually run.
- Walk around for 5-10 minutes
- If you have time, walk around the staging area, read your jokes, laugh, relax
- Get in position and pick one side of the road or the other where you want to line up.
- When the road is closed, and participants are called onto the road, go to the curb and stay at the side of the road, near or at the back of the crowd.

After the start

Remember that you can control how you feel during and afterward by conservative pacing from the beginning—and walk breaks. Be sure to move over to the side of the road to take walk breaks.

- Stick with your run/walk ratio that has worked for you—take every walk break, especially the first one
- If it is warm, slow down and walk more (30 sec/mi slower for each 5°F above 60°F/20 sec/km for each 2°C above 14°C)
- Don't let yourself be pulled out too fast in the beginning—which is so easy to do.
- As people pass you who aren't taking walk breaks, tell yourself that you will catch them later—you will.
- If anyone interprets your walking as weakness, say: "I feel good and finish strong when I do this."
- Talk with folks along the way, enjoy the course, smile often

- On warm days, pour water over your head at the water stops, drinking no more than 27 oz an hour (no need to drink on a 5K unless you want to).

At the finish
- In the upright position
- With a smile on your face
- Wanting to do it again

After the finish
- Keep walking for at least half a mile
- Drink about 4-8 oz of fluid
- Within 30 minutes of the finish, have a snack that is 80% carbohydrate/20% protein (Endurox R4 is best)
- If you can soak your legs in cool water for 10 + minutes, during the first two hours after the race, do so
- Walk for 20-30 minutes later in the day

The next day
- Walk for 30-60 minutes, very easy. This can be done at one time, or in installments
- Keep drinking about 4-6 oz an hour of water or a sports drink like Accelerade
- Go back to your usual schedule of running/walking—every other day—but exercise more easily.
- Wait at least a week before you either schedule your next race or vow to never run another one.

Stretching

It may surprise you to learn this, but stretching causes a lot of injuries. Our surveys have found that among those who stretch regularly, stretching is the leading cause of injury. While there are some specific stretches that help some individuals, we believe that most people who run don't need to stretch at all. Yes, you'll get a lot of advice to stretch—especially from those who are involved in other activities like tennis, swimming, soccer, golf, etc. Recreational distance running is significantly different than those other activities.

In other sports, you are asking your body to do what it was not designed to do. Our ancient ancestors didn't play tennis or golf. But they did walk....and run. If we do these two activities gently, as noted in this book, we will stay within the ranges of motion for which we were designed. Stretching pushes the tendons and muscles beyond what they are currently ready to do, and often pushes them into injury.

Tightness

Don't be alarmed by the tightness you receive from running as you increase the distance. On an individual run, most of the tightness comes from muscle fatigue, and the waste products that are deposited as you continue to extend the distance. Stretching will not take away this type of tightness. Nor will stretching remove the tightness that naturally occurs as you get older.

A false sense of relief We fully admit that if you stretch a tired, tight muscle, it feels better...for a short period. After talking to dozens of physiologists, orthopedists, and other specialists, we've come to understand that stretching a tight muscle produces many small tears of the muscle fibers. Your body senses this and sends hormones to kill the pain. Even one stretch under these conditions can injure a muscle and definitely increases recovery time as your body repairs the stretching damage. Even with light stretching, you will weaken the muscle.

Some tightness is good Your body will get a bit tighter as you run, for a while. This is due to the legs adapting to a more efficient motion. We've been told by many bio-mechanics experts that this type of tightness, in most cases, reduces the chance of injury and makes running more natural.

If you are having a problem with tightness in a certain part of the body, massage can help—even using the self-help massage tools, such as "the stick". A longer and more gentle warm-up will also reduce tightness. You can also consult the landmark book on this subject STRETCHING, by Bob Anderson.

Yoga and Pilates?

We communicate with runners and walkers about every week, who get injured because they stretched during these programs. Even mild stretches that are outside your range of motion can be adverse to the joints, and tendons.

Ilio-tibial band injury—the only major exception

The ilio-tibial band is composed of interlocking fascia that acts as a tendon. It starts at the hip and continues along the outside of each leg, attaching in several places below the knee. Besides the stretch noted here, individuals find that there are specific stretches that will help to release the tightness of their I-T band. Those who suffer from this injury can stretch before, after, or during a run-walk, or whenever it tightens up and/or starts to hurt. There is more on this injury in the injury section of this book.

Don't feel guilty if you don't stretch before you run-walk

A gentle walk for 5 minutes, followed by a very gradual transition from walking to run-walk has been the most effective warm up that we've found.

If you have individual stretches that work....DO THEM!

We've met several people who have certain stretches that seem to help them. If you find a stretch that works for you, go ahead. Just be careful.

Strengthening

There are a few strengthening activities that can help your running or walking. But we don't believe that running is a strength activity. As noted in the "form" chapters, the running motion uses momentum and inertia. Once you get your body into motion with a few steps, simply maintain that momentum.

Just look at the leg muscle development of faster distance runners. It is minimal. Carrying around extra superstructure that doesn't help you move forward is extra work for the body—causing a slowdown later in a long run.

The following exercises are not meant to be prescriptions for medical problems. They are offered from one exerciser to another because thousands have reported benefit from them. If you have a back or other medical issue, make sure your doctor and other specialists give you permission to use these exercises.

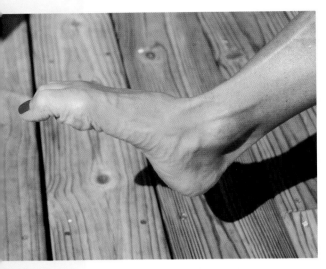

Toe squincher

—for prevention of injuries of the foot and lower leg—such as plantar fasciia

We believe that this exercise will help every person that runs and walks. Whether barefooted or not, point your toes and contract the muscles of your foot until they cramp. It only takes a few seconds for this to happen. You can repeat this exercise 10-30 times a day, every day.

Postural muscle exercises

By balancing the strength of muscles on the upper body that maintain your posture, you'll tend to be more upright and balanced whether running, walking or standing. Well-toned postural muscles will also allow for more efficient breathing—reducing the chance of side pain. There are two areas to be strengthened.

Front muscles: the crunch

Lie on your back on a cushioned carpet or floor pad with adequate cushioning for your back. Bend your knees. Now raise your head and upper back very slightly off the floor. Go up an inch or two and down, but don't let the upper back hit the floor. As you move very slightly, don't let the stomach muscles relax—keep them working as you go up and down in this very narrow range of motion. It also helps, as you are doing this, to roll slightly to either side, continuously moving. This strengthens the whole range of muscle groups that support the front side of your torso.

For the back, shoulders and neck: arm running

Holding a dumbbell in each hand, while standing (not while running), go through a range of motion that is a bit greater than you would use when running/walking. Keep the weights close to your body as the hands swing from your waist up to your shoulders, and return.

Pick a weight that makes you feel, after a set of 10 repetitions, that you got a workout out of the muscles involved. But don't have so much weight that you have to struggle as you get your last 1-2 reps. Start with one set of 10, and increase to 3-5 sets, once or twice a week. This can be done on a run day, or on a rest day.

Prescriptive exercises

These are designed for those who feel that they need more support in one or more of the areas listed below. Those who have had regular aches, pains or injuries in one of the areas below have received benefit from these exercises.

Knees—the stiff leg lift

If you have weak knees, this exercise can strengthen the various muscles in the thigh. By developing strength in the range of muscles above, you may tighten the connections around the knee, providing better support.

Sit on a tall bench or table. With a stiff leg, lift the leg up and down, gradually changing the range of motion from inside to outside. Start with no weight, and one set of 10 lifts. When you can easily do 3 sets of 10 lifts with each leg, add a few pounds using a bag or pocketbook, looped around the ankle.

Shins—2 exercises

The foot lift

Sit on a bench, with knee bent at a right angle. Your foot must be significantly off the floor. Hang a bag or pocket book with a pound of weight over the foot. Lift your foot up and down 10 times. Move the angle of the foot to the inside and the outside. Add more weight when a set of 10 feels easy.

Heel walking

Use a very padded shoe. Walk on your heels so that your toe region is off the floor. Start with 10 steps, and increase until you can do 2-3 sets of 20-30 steps.

#27

Cross-training: Getting Better as You Rest the Legs

If you enjoy an exercise boost every day, variety can invigorate your training program. It's particularly important for women who've had stress fractures to alternate between pounding exercises such as running, and non-impact activities: swimming, cycling, and water running. Progress is made more quickly when there is enough rest time between workouts (usually 48 hours) to allow for rebuilding of muscles, tendons, etc. Cross-training can be done on the "rest" days between running/walking days. Walking at a gentle pace usually does not produce enough damage to require a day of rest— except for those with bone density problems and other issues. It is usually best, however, to rest the day before long runs.

Cross-training activities

Cross training simply means "alternative exercise". Almost any exercise will make you feel better and helps to boost your health potential. Most of these alternative exercises don't deliver the same attitude boost as runners feel after a run. You will be burning calories and fat as you relieve stress.

WHEN YOU START ANY EXERCISE (OR ARE STARTING BACK, AFTER A LAYOFF):

1. Start with 5 easy minutes of exercise, rest for 20 or more minutes and do 5 more easy minutes.
2. Take a day of rest between this exercise (you can do a different exercise the next day).
3. Increase by 2-3 additional minutes each segment until you get to the number of minutes that gives you the appropriate feeling of exertion.
4. Once you have increased to two 15-minute sessions, you could shift to one 22-25-minute session and increase by 2-3 more minutes per session if you wish.
5. It's best to do no exercise the day before a long run, a very hard speed session, or a race.
6. To maintain your conditioning in each alternative exercise, do one session each week of 10 minutes or more, once you reach that amount. If you have the time, you can cross-train (XT) on all of your days off from running—except listed in #5 above.
7. The maximum amount of cross-training is up to the individual. As long as you are feeling fine for the rest of the day and having no trouble with your run the next day, the length of your cross-training should not be a problem.

Water running can improve your running form

All runners have flips and side motions that reduce running efficiency. During a water running workout, the resistance of the water forces your legs to find a more efficient path. In addition, several leg muscles are strengthened which can help keep your legs

on a smoother path when they get tired at the end of a long run. Water running is the best cross training mode for runners that we've found.

Here's how!

You'll need a flotation belt for this exercise. The product "Aqua Jogger" is designed to float you off the bottom of the pool. Pull in the elastic belt so that it fits snugly. While some water runners do so without a belt, most find it easier to use some form of floatation. Get in the deep end of the pool and move your legs through a running motion. This means little or no knee lift, kicking out slightly in front of you, and bringing the leg behind, with the foot coming up slightly behind you. As in running, your lower leg should be parallel with the horizontal during the back-kick.

If you are not feeling much exertion, you're probably lifting the knees too high and moving your legs through a small range of motion. To get the benefit, an extended running motion is needed.

It's important to do water running once a week to keep the adaptations that you have gained. If you miss a week, you should drop back a few minutes from your previous session. If you miss more than 3 weeks, start back at two 5-8 min sessions.

Fat burning and overall fitness exercises

Nordic track
This exercise simulates the motion used in cross-country skiing. It is one of the best cross-training modes for fat burning because it allows you to use a great number of muscle cells while raising body temperature. If you exercise at an easy pace, you can get into the fat burning zone (past 45 minutes) after a gradual buildup to that amount.

Rowing machine
While some rowing machines work the legs a bit too hard (on a rest day from running), most allow you to use a wide variety of lower and upper body muscle groups. This is a good fat-burning exercise.

Cycling
Indoor cycling (on an exercise cycle) is a better fat-burner exercise than outdoor cycling, because it raises your body temperature a bit higher. The muscles used in both indoor and outdoor cycling are mostly the quadraceps—on the front of the thigh—reducing the total number of muscle cells compared with rowing, Nordic Track, etc.

Don't forget walking!
Walking can be done all day long. I call walking a "stealthy fat-burner" exercise because it is so easy to add hundreds of extra steps a day—especially in small doses. Walking is also an excellent cross training exercise. Caution: Don't walk with a long stride.

Cross-training for the upper body

Weight training for the bones
While weight work is not a great fat-burning exercise, it can be done on non-running days, or on run day, after a workout. There are a wide range of different ways to build strength. Strength training workouts can be designed to help bolster connections to the spine, and other crucial structures. As mentioned previously in this book, weight training for the legs is not recommended.

Get advice before beginning weight training

It pays to spend an hour with an experienced strength training expert, who can design a program based upon your problems and capabilities. Get advice from an expert before trying any strengthening exercises, including the ones mentioned in this book.

Postural muscle strengthening—can help prevent osteoporosis

To reduce the leaning and slumping of the upper body, it helps to build up the muscles that help you stay upright. The two exercises I use are listed below. Exercises that have helped with spinal connections are the following: arm running, shoulder shrug, upright rowing and bench press. Before doing any exercise, get advice from a physical therapist or knowledgeable strength trainer. Be sure to tell that person about any back or other problems you may have.

The crunch—lie on your back, on carpet or any padded surface. Lift your head and upper back slightly off the floor. Go through a narrow range of motion so that you feel your abdominal muscles contracting almost constantly. Start with a few seconds of these, and build up to 30-60 seconds, done 3-5 times a day (one or two days a week)

Arm running—while standing, with hand held weights (milk jugs, etc.) move your arms through a wide range of motion you would use when running—maybe slightly more than usual. Keep the weights close to the body. Start with a few reps, and gradually build up to 3-5 sets of 10. Pick a weight that is challenging enough so that you feel exertion at the end of a set of 10, but you don't want to have to struggle during the last few reps.

Swimming

While not a fat-burner, swimming strengthens the upper body, while it promotes cardiovascular fitness and endurance in those muscles. Swimming can be done on both running days and non-running days.

Push-ups and pull-ups
These can build upper body strength as you innovate to work the upper body muscle groups you want to strengthen.

DON'T DO THESE ON NON-RUNNING DAYS!
The following exercises will tire the running muscles and compromise recovery. If you really like to do any of these exercises, you can do them after a run on a short-distance day. Avoid these completely if you have any pains in the knee or shin.

- Stair machines
- Step aerobics (can cause knee problems)
- Weight training for the leg muscles
- Power walking—especially on a hilly course
- Spinning classes (on a bicycle) in which you stand up on the pedals and push

Cross-training can keep you fit, if you must stop running
I know of many runners who have had to take 2 weeks off from running or more, and have not lost noticeable fitness. How? They cross-trained. As noted above, the most effective cross-training mode for runners is water running.

The key is to do an activity (like water running) that uses the same range of motion used in running/walking. This keeps the neuromuscular system working to capacity (water running is best).

To maintain conditioning, you must simulate the time and the effort level you would have spent when running. For example, if you were scheduled for a long run/walk that would have taken you 60 minutes, get in the pool and run for 60 minutes. You can take segments of 40-60 seconds in which you reduce your effort (like a walk break), every few minutes to keep the muscles resilient.

Dealing with the Heat

Exercising in the heat is not only difficult, it can be dangerous. The heart has to work harder when it is hot—even when running slower. Check with your doctor if you have any questions about your risk in this area.

Avoid heat disease. When you exercise strenuously in even moderate heat (above 60°F), you'll raise core body temperature triggering a release of blood into the capillaries of your skin to cool you down. This diversion reduces the blood supply available to your exercising muscles. With less blood and oxygen delivered to the power source, your heart and many other crucial whole body organism must work harder and you feel bad. As the waste builds up in the muscle, you will slow down. Make sure that you read the section on this health problem at the end of this chapter.

Preventive slowdown or ending the workout is best. But it is always better to back off or stop running/walking at the first sign that you may be coming into this condition. The following are proven ways of avoiding heat adversity.

Working out during summer heat

Run/walk before the sun gets above the horizon. Get up early during the warm months and you will avoid most of the extra stress from the radiant effect of the sun. This is particularly a problem in humid areas. Early morning is usually the coolest time of the day. Without having to deal with the sun, most runners/walkers can gradually adapt to heat. At the very least, your workouts will be more enjoyable than those done later in the day.

Note: Be sure to take care of safety issues.

- If you must run/walk outdoors when the sun is up, pick a shady course. Shade provides a significant relief in areas of low humidity, and some relief in humid environments.

- In areas of low humidity, it's usually cool during the evening and night. In humid environments there may not be much relief. The coolest time of the day when it's humid is just before dawn.

- Have an indoor facility available. If you use treadmills, you can exercise in air conditioning. If a treadmill bores you, alternate segments of 5-10 minutes—one segment outdoor, and the next indoor.

- Don't wear a hat! You lose most of your body heat through the top of your head. Covering the head will cause a quicker internal buildup of heat.

- Wear light clothing, but not cotton. Many of the new, technical fibers (Dryscience, Polypro, Coolmax, Drifit, etc.) will move moisture away from your skin, producing a cooling effect. Cotton soaks up the sweat, making the garment heavier as it sticks to your skin. This means that you won't receive as much of a cooling effect as that provided by the tech products.

- Pour water over your head. Evaporation not only helps the cooling process—it makes you feel cooler. This psychological boost can make a big difference in motivation, and may help you complete a difficult workout. You can freeze a plastic water bottle overnight, and carry it with you on your walk/run.

- Run/walk the short workouts in installments. It is fine, on a short distance assignment, on a hot day, to put in your 30 minutes by doing 10 in the morning, 10 at noon and 10 at night. The long one, however, should be done at one time.

- Take a pool break, or a shower chill-down. During a run, it really helps to take a 2-4 minute dip in a pool or a shower. Some runners in hot areas run loops around their neighborhood and let the hose run over their head each lap. The pool is especially helpful in soaking out excess body temperature. I have run in 97 degree temperatures at our Florida running retreat, breaking up a 5-mile run into 3 x 1.7 mi. Between each, I take a 2-3 minute "soak break" in the pool and get back out there. It was only at the end of each segment that I got warm again.

- Sun screen—a mixed review. Some runners will need to protect themselves. Some products, however, produce a coating on the skin, slowing down the perspiration and producing an increase in body temperature buildup. If you are only in the sun for 30-50 minutes at a time, you may not need to put on sunscreen for cancer protection. Consult with a dermatologist for your specific needs—or find a product that doesn't block the pores.

- Drink 6-8 oz of a sports drink like Accelerade or water, at least every 2 hours, or when thirsty, throughout the day (not when running/walking) during hot weather. Cold water is the best beverage for most, according to my experience, during a hot workout. Recommended fluid intake is no more than 14-27 oz an hour during exercise.

- Look at the clothing thermometer at the end of this section. Wear loose fitting garments, that have some texture in the fabric. Texture will limit or prevent the perspiration from causing a clinging effect that limits the coolness of evaporation.

- When the temperature is above 90°F, you have my permission to re-arrange your shoes—preferably in an air-conditioned environment.

Hot weather slowdown for runners on long endurance workouts

As the temperature rises above 55°F (12°C), your body starts to build up heat, but most runners/walkers aren't significantly slowed until 60°F (14°C). If you make the adjustments early, you won't have to suffer later and slow down a lot more at that time. The baseline for this table is 60°F or 14°C.

Runners: 30 seconds a mile slower for every 5 degree increase above 60°F (20 sec/kilometer slower for every 2 degrees above 14°C).

HEAT DISEASE ALERT !

While it is unlikely that you will push yourself into heat disease, the longer you are exercising in hot (and/or humid) conditions, the more you increase the likelihood of this dangerous medical situation. That's why I recommend breaking up your short runs into short segments when it's hot, if you must run outdoors. Be sensitive to your reactions to the heat, and those of the runners/walkers around you. When one of the symptoms is present, this is normally not a major problem unless there is significant distress. But when 2 or more are experienced, take action because heat disease can lead to death. It's always better to be conservative: stop the workout, cool off, and get help immediately, if needed.

Those who have cardiovascular disease, who have symptoms and a family history of it, or who have significant risk factors should avoid hot weather running completely (use a treadmill). Walking may be OK—check with your doctor.

Symptoms of heat disease

(Stop exercising if you experience 2 or more of these)
- Intense heat build-up in the head
- General overheating of the body
- Significant headache
- Significant nausea
- General confusion and loss of concentration
- Loss of muscle control
- Excessive sweating and then cessation of sweating
- Clammy skin
- Excessively rapid breathing
- Muscle cramps
- Feeling faint
- Unusual heart beat or rhythm

Heat disease risk factors

- Viral or bacterial infection
- Taking medication—especially cold medicines, diruretics, medicines for diarrhea, antihistamines, atropine, scopamine, tranquilizers, even cholesterol and blood pressure medications. Check with your doctor on medication issues—especially when running in hot weather.
- Dehydration (especially due to alcohol)
- Severe sunburn
- Overweight
- Lack of heat training
- Exercising more than one is used to
- Occurrence of heat disease in the past
- Two or more nights of extreme sleep deprivation
- Certain medical conditions including high cholesterol, high

blood pressure, extreme stress, asthma, diabetes, epilepsy, cardiovascular disease, smoking, or a general lack of fitness
• Drug use, including alcohol, over-the-counter medications, prescription drugs, etc. (consult with your doctor about using drugs when you are exercising in hot weather)

Hyponatremia—dangerous consumption of too much water
If you're running/walking more than 4 hours and are drinking more than 27 oz of fluid, you could be producing a dangerous depletion of sodium that could lead to death. Women are much more prone to this condition than men, possibly because they tend to drink more fluid for their body weight than men. Symptoms of this condition include the following, but none may be present:
• swelling of hands (to twice normal size)
• cramping in legs
• significant loss of concentration
• diarrhea or vomiting—if exercising for more than 4 hours and suffering from either, get help immediately

Here's how to prevent this dangerous condition:
• Drink no more than 27 oz of fluid an hour
• Avoid taking anti-inflammatory medication before or during a run of more than 4 hours
• Talk to your doctor about any medication you are taking—mentioning hyponatremia and that you plan to run more than 4 hours. Follow the doctor's advice concerning medication issues
• If you cramp regularly, ask your doctor if you can take a salt tablet during exercise (Succeed is a good one).

Take action! Call 911
Use your best judgement, but in most cases anyone who exhibits two or more of the symptoms should get into a cool environment, and get medical attention immediately. An extremely effective cool-off method is to soak towels, sheets or clothing in cool or cold water, and wrap them around the individual. If ice is available, sprinkle some ice over the wet cloth.

Problems/Solutions

Troubleshooting Performance

Nauseous at the end of runs

- You ran too fast at the beginning
- Temperature is above 65°F/17°C (slow down by 30 sec/mi for every 5°F or 20 sec/km for every 2°C above 14°C)
- You ate too much (or drank too much) before the race or workout—even hours before
- You ate the wrong foods—most commonly fat, fried foods, milk products, fibrous foods
- You ate or drank too much during the run
- Since sports drinks cause nausea during runs, use water for your fluid replacement

Tired during workouts

Here are the possible reasons—see your doctor for more help.

- Low in B vitamins
- Low in iron—have a serum ferritin test, and cook food in an iron skillet
- Not eating enough protein
- Blood sugar is low before exercise—eat more often during the day, and have a snack 30-60 minutes before
- Not eating within 30 minutes of the finish of a previous run (to re-stock muscle glycogen)
- Eating too much fat—especially before or right after a run
- Running too many days per week
- Running too hard on long runs
- Working too hard on all exercise days
- Not taking enough walk breaks (shuffle breaks) from the beginning of your runs/walks

REASONS WHY YOU MAY NOT BE IMPROVING:

- You're over-trained, and tired—if so, reduce your training, and/or take an extra rest day
- You may have chosen a goal that is too ambitious for your current ability
- You may have missed some of your workouts, or not been as regular with your training
- The temperature may have been above 60°F (14°C). Above this, you will slow down (the longer the race, the greater the effect of increased heat).
- When using different test courses, one of them may not have been accurately measured.
- You ran the first third of the workout or the race, too fast.

Side pain

This is very common, and usually has a simple fix. Normally it is nothing to worry about...it just hurts. This condition is due to 1) the lack of deep breathing, and 2) going a little too fast from the beginning of the run. You can correct #2 easily by walking more at the beginning, and/or slowing down your pace from the beginning.

Deep breathing from the beginning of a run can prevent side pain. This way of inhaling air is performed by diverting the air you breathe into your lower lungs. Also called "belly breathing", this is how we breathe when asleep, and it provides maximum opportunity for oxygen absorption. If you don't deep-breathe when you run, and you are not getting the oxygen you need, the side pain will tell you. By slowing down, walking, and breathing deeply for a while, the pain may go away. But sometimes it does not. Most runners just continue to run with the side pain. In 50 years of running and helping others run, I've not seen any lasting negative effect due to common side pain—it just hurts.

You don't have to take a maximum breath to perform this technique. Simply breathe a normal breath but send it to the lower lungs. You know that you have done this if your stomach goes up and down as you inhale and exhale. If your chest goes up and down, you are breathing shallowly.

Note: Never breathe in and out rapidly. This can lead to hyperventilation, dizziness, and fainting.

Blisters & black toenails

Blisters are caused by the constant rubbing of a particular place on the foot or toe. Black toenails are, in effect, a blister underneath the toenail. Both can be the result of shoes that are too tight, and most commonly occur when the foot has experienced swelling due to heat and distance. With some help from a good running store, you can get a good fitting shoe, providing about half to three-quarters of an inch of extra room at the end of your larger big toe. Lace the shoe so that the foot is comfortable but not too loose.

There are several spots on your feet where blisters will tend to occur. Eventually you'll develop thicker skin on these areas, and natural adaptations. On hot days, you'll reduce the chance of blisters if you'll put foot powder in the shoe and the sock, and put a light smear of Vasoline or "Glide" on the potential hot spots.

Most of the black toe nails experienced by my eCoach clients and myself seem to be due to internal fluid buildup on long runs and hot days. As your foot comes forward with each step you sling a little more fluid into the toe region. Thousands of steps later, as you push back the distance of your long run, you can produce a pressure underneath the big toe that leads to the rupture of some blood capillaries in that area. When this happens, even a small amount of blood will cause the toenail to look dark red or black.

While the pressure may cause some temporary pain, this is not a serious problem. Usually the fluid is just underneath the toenail and can be released with a sterilized needle at the edge of the nail when fluid is present there. If the fluid is underneath the toenail, many runners will release it by heating the end of a paper clip with a match until red, and melting a small hole in the center of toenail to release the pocket of fluid. In all cases with blisters, it is best to immediately apply or insert some triple antibiotic cream into the opening.

I feel great one day...and not the next

If you can solve this problem, you could become a very wealthy person. There are a few common reasons for this, but there will always be "those days" when the body doesn't seem to work right, or the gravity seems stronger than normal—and you cannot find a reason. You should keep looking for the causes of your letdowns in your journal. If you feel this way several times a week, for two or more weeks in a row, you may need more rest in your program—or may need a medical checkup.

1. Just do it. In most cases, this is a one-day occurrence. Most exercisers just put more easy walking/shuffling into the mix, slow down, and get through it. Before doing a challenging

workout, however, make sure that there's not a medical reason for the "bad" feeling. I've had some of my best workouts after feeling very bad during the first few miles because I did not stop.

2. Heat and/or humidity will make you feel worse. You will often feel better when the temperature is below 60°F (14°C) and miserable when 75°F (21.5°C) or above—and/or the humidity is high.

3. Low blood sugar can make you feel bad during any run. You may feel good at the start and suddenly feel like you have no energy. Every step seems to take a major effort. Read the section in this book on blood sugar.

4. Low motivation. Use the rehearsal techniques in the "mental toughness" chapter to get you out the door on a bad day—or to help you continue on a tough day. These have helped numerous runners turn their minds around—even in the middle of exercise.

5. Infection can leave you feeling lethargic, achy, and unable to run at the same pace that was easy a few days earlier. Check the normal signs (fever, chills, swollen lymph glands, higher morning pulse rate, etc.) and at least call your doctor if you suspect something.

6. Medication and alcohol, even when taken the day before, can leave a hangover that may not affect any area of your life except for your running. Your doctor or pharmacist should be able to tell you about the effect of medication on strenuous exercise.

7. A slower start can make the difference between a good day and a bad day. When your body is on the edge of fatigue or other stress, just 5-10 seconds too fast per mile can push into discomfort or worse. A quick adjustment to a slower pace before you get too tired can turn this around.

8. Caffeine can help because it gets the central nervous system working to top capacity. I feel better and my legs work so much better when I have had a cup of coffee an hour before the start of a run. Of course, those who have any problems with caffeine should avoid it.

9. Take an extra day off each week—especially if you're running 4 or more days per week.

10. If the fatigue continues for more than 5 days, and you have adjusted other items above, you should talk to your doctor and possibly get some blood work done. You may be low in iron, B vitamins or other nutrients.

Cramps in the muscles

Most runners experience at least some cramping. These muscle contractions usually occur in the feet or the calf muscles and may come during a run, or they may hit at random afterward. Most commonly, they will occur at night, or when you are sitting around at your desk or watching TV in the afternoon or evening. When severe cramps occur during a run, you will have to stop or significantly slow down.

Cramps vary in severity. Most are mild but some can grab so hard that they shut down the muscles and hurt when they seize up. Significant reduction in the effort level, relaxing the muscle, with light massage can help to bring most of the cramps around. Odds are that stretching will make the cramp worse, or tear the muscle fibers.

Most cramps are due to overuse—doing more than in the recent past, or continuing to put yourself at your limit, especially in warm weather. Look at the pace and distance of your runs in your training journal to see if you have been going too far, or too fast, or both. A high percentage of muscle cramps that are reported to me each year are due to training too fast when the temperature rises above 60°F or 14°C.

- Remember to adjust pace for heat: slow down 30 seconds a mile for each 5 degrees (F) of temperature increase above 60°F—or 20 sec/kilometer for every 2 degrees C of temperature increase above 14°F (see "hot weather slowdown" section in the last chapter). You can always slow down more than this.

- Continuous running and walking increases the chance of cramping especially in warm weather. Taking walk breaks (shuffle breaks) more often can reduce or eliminate them. Many runners who used to cramp when they ran continuously, eliminated cramps by inserting a 1-minute walk break after 1-3 minutes of running during long runs. Runners who cramped at 3-1(run 3 minutes/walk 1 minute), have often avoided cramping using 1-1 or 2-1.

- During hot weather, a good electrolyte beverage (consumed throughout the day as your beverage of choice) can help to replace the salts that your body loses in sweating. A drink like Accelerade, for example, can help to restock these minerals when you drink @ 6-8 oz every 1-2 hours, throughout the day.

- On very long hikes, walks or runs, continuous sweating (especially when drinking a lot of fluid) can push your sodium levels too low and produce muscle cramping. If this happens regularly, a buffered salt tablet has helped greatly—a product like Succeed. Check with your doctor first.

- Many medications, especially those designed to lower cholesterol, have muscle cramps as one of their known side effects. Runners who use medications and suffer from cramps should ask their doctor about this issue and investigate alternatives.

Dealing with cramps
1. Take a longer and more gentle warmup
2. Runners: Shorten your run segment, increase the walk segment—or take walk breaks more often
3. Shorten your distance on a hot/humid day

4. Break your daily distance into two segments (but not long ones)
5. Look at any other exercise that could be causing the cramps
6. Take a buffered salt tablet at the beginning of your exercise
7. Don't push off as hard, or bounce as high off the ground
8. If you are exercising two days or more in a row, shift to an every-other-day pattern.

Note: Ask your doctor before taking any salt supplement.

Upset stomach or diarrhea

Sooner or later, virtually every runner has at least one episode of exercise-related nausea or diarrhea. It comes from the buildup of total stress that you accumulate in your life—and specifically the stress of the workout. But stress is the result of many unique conditions within the individual. Your body produces the nausea/diarrhea to get you to reduce the intensity of the exercise, which will reduce the stress. Here are the common causes.

1. *Running too fast or running too far* is the most common cause. Exercisers are confused about this, because the pace doesn't feel too fast in the beginning. Each person has a level of fatigue that triggers these conditions. Slowing down and taking more walk breaks will help you manage the problem.

2. *Eating too much or too soon before the run.* Your system has to work hard when running, and it is also hard work to digest food. Doing both at the same time raises stress and results in nausea, etc. Having food in your stomach, in the process of being digested, is an extra stress and a likely target for elimination.

3. *Eating a diet high in fat or protein*. Even one meal that has over 50% of the calories in fat or protein can lead to nausea/diarrhea (N/D) hours later—when you run.

4. *Eating too much the afternoon or evening, the day before.* A big evening meal will still be in the gut the next morning, being digested. When you bounce up and down on a run, you add stress to the system, sometimes resulting in N/D.

5. *Heat and humidity are a major cause of these problems.* Some people don't adapt well to even modest heat increases and experience N/D when running at the same pace that did not produce the problem in cool weather. In hot conditions, everyone has a core body temperature increase that will result in significant stress to the system—often causing nausea, and sometimes diarrhea. By slowing down, taking more walk breaks, and pouring water over your head, you can manage this better.

6. *Drinking too much water before a run.* If you have too much water in your stomach, and you are bouncing around, you put stress on the digestive system. Reduce your intake to the bare minimum. Most runners don't need to drink any fluid before a workout that is 60 minutes or less.

7. *Drinking too much of a sugar/electrolyte drink.* Water is the easiest substance for the body to process. The addition of sugar and/or electrolyte minerals, as in a sports drink, makes the substance harder to digest. During a run (especially on a hot day) it is best to drink only water if you have had N/D or other problems. Cold water is best. But even too much water can upset the system.

8. *Drinking too much fluid (especially a sugar drink) too soon after a workout.* Even if you are very thirsty, don't gulp down large quantities of any fluid during a short period of time after exercise. Try to drink no more than 6-8 oz, every 20 minutes or so. If you are particularly prone to N/D, just take 2-4 sips, every 5 minutes or so. When the body is very stressed and tired, and you've had N/D after workouts before, it's not a good idea to consume a sugar drink (sports drink, etc.) within 20 minutes of your finish.

9. ***Don't let the workout be stressful to you.*** Some exercisers get too obsessed about getting their workout in or maintaining at a specific pace. This adds stress to your life. Relax and let the exercise diffuse some of the other tensions in your life. When you are under a lot of "life stress" it's OK to delay a workout when the thought of it increases your stress level. You can also decrease the intensity. You should be in charge—not some training schedule. If you are experiencing frequent N/D without cause, see your physician.

Headache

There are several reasons why exercisers get workout-induced headaches. While uncommon, they happen to the average runner about 1-5 times a year. The extra stress that exercise puts on the body can trigger a headache on a tough day—even considering the relaxation that comes afterward. Many runners find that one dose of an over-the-counter headache medication takes care of the problem. As always, consult with your doctor about use of medication. Here are some of the causes/solutions:

Dehydration—if you exercise in the morning, make sure that you hydrate well the day before. Avoid alcohol if you work out in the mornings and have headaches. Also watch the salt in your dinner meal the night before (or too much salt all day long) if you are experiencing headaches. A good sports drink like Accelerade, taken throughout the day the day before, will help to keep your fluid levels and your electrolytes "topped off". If you run in the afternoon, follow the same advice leading up to your exercise session. If you are dehydrated an hour before a workout, it doesn't help to drink a huge amount of water at that time—6-8 oz is fine.

Medications can often produce dehydration—there are some medications that make exercisers more prone to dehydration-related headaches. Check with your doctor.

Too hot for you—schedule your workout at a cooler time of the day (usually in the morning before the sun gets above the horizon). When on a hot run, pour water over your head. Try to find shady courses or use a treadmill on hot days.

Being in the sun—try to stay in the shade as much as possible. Wear a visor (not a hat), making sure the band is not too tight. When the temperature rises above 60°F, don't cover the top of your head.

Exercising too hard—start all workouts more slowly, and keep the pace slower on hot days.

Going further than you have, in the recent past—monitor your mileage and don't increase more than about 15% further than you have gone on any single run in the recent past. When increasing (or when doing any long one) be sure to slow down: runners should run at least 2 min/mi slower than you could legitimately run for a marathon (see the "magic mile" segment in this book).

Low blood sugar level—be sure that you boost your BSL with a snack, about 30-60 minutes before your workout. If you are used to having it, caffeine in a beverage can sometimes help this situation also—but caffeine causes headaches for a small percentage of exercisers.

If prone to migranes—generally avoid caffeine, and try your best to avoid dehydration. Talk to your doctor about other possibilities.

Watch your neck and lower back—If you lean forward as you run, you can put pressure on the spine—particularly in the neck and lower back. Read the form chapter in this book and run upright.

30

Injury Troubleshooting (as one exerciser to another)

The various types of doctors

Try to find a specialist that wants to get you back exercising as soon as is realistic. Ask around at the local running stores in the hopes of finding someone who has treated a lot of runners with the same problem you have, successfully.

Orthopedist—specialist in the leg, foot, back, etc. They can provide the widest range of diagnosis and treatment.

Podiatrist—specializes in the foot, and in leg injuries that are caused by action of the foot (such as knee problems caused when the foot rolls to the inside). This specialist is trained in the science of orthotics to correct such extra motion. I don't recommend jumping right into a serious orthotic at the first sign of a knee or other problem. Usually the problem can be corrected with minor adjustments in shoes, medication, and training.

Massage Therapist—a very experienced practitioner can often identify problems, and sometimes can work them out, in a series of sessions. Deep tissue massage, when needed, can restore muscles to a normal range of function.

Physical Therapist—specializes in rehabilitation of injured areas using stretching, strengthening, muscle manipulation and other treatments.

Chiropractor—Some of my eCoach clients who could not find successful back treatment with other doctors have had some success with this specialist, but treatment options are much more limited.

Accupuncture—can manage pain, allowing some use of the injured area, in many cases. Generally this is not a long-term treatment mode, in my opinion

Quick treatment tips

For all injuries
- Take 3 days off from running or any activity that could aggravate the area
- As you return to exercise, stay below the threshold of further irritation with an easier effort
- Don't stretch unless you have ilio-tibial band injury. Stretching interferes with the healing of most injuries—and often increases the healing time.

Muscle injuries
- Call your doctor's office and see if you can take prescription-strength anti-inflammatory medication. Always follow your doctor's advice about medication.
- See a sports massage therapist who has worked successfully on many exercisers—especially runners—deep tissue massage can speed up muscle recovery.

- If you experience no improvement after 4 days of no exercise, call an orthopedist who wants to get you back working out as soon as possible, and set up an appointment.

Tendon and foot injuries

- Rub a chunk of ice directly on the area for 15 minutes every night (keep rubbing until the area gets numb—about 15 minutes) Note: ice bags, or gel ice don't seem to do any good at all.
- Foot injuries sometimes are helped by an air cast at first. This can stabilize the foot or leg so that the healing can begin.

Knee injuries

- Call your doctor's office to see if you can take prescription strength anti-inflammatory medication
- Try very gentle walking, for a week or two. Sometimes this will allow the knee to heal while maintaining a lot of the conditioning.
- Sometimes knee bands & straps (available at many running stores) can relieve pain—ask your doctor. In most cases, you must try these to see if they help.
- Get a shoe check to see if you are wearing the right pair (if you over-pronate, a motion control shoe may help).
- If you over-pronate, an orthotic may help—but try other options before investing in a serious orthotic.
- If you have internal knee pain, glucosamine supplements may help (usually takes 6-8 weeks to take effect).

Shin injuries

- See a doctor if there are any signs of a stress fracture. The most common stress fracture symptom is that the shin pain gets worse as you run—but check with your doctor. You should not do any weight-bearing exercise if you have any type of fracture—get your doctor's advice before proceeding with training.
- If the pain gradually goes away as you run on it, there is less worry of a stress fracture—but this is not a foolproof test. In most cases, when the pain goes away during exercise, you have a shin splint. If you stay below the threshold of activity that irritates the

shin muscle, you can exercise with shin splints, as they are less and less of an issue (check with doctor to be sure).

- Take more walk breaks, go more slowly, etc.

Exercising while healing

With most injuries, you can continue to work out while the injury is healing. But first, you must take some time away from the activity to get the healing started. If you do this at the beginning of an injury, only 2-5 days may be needed. The longer you continue to train, the more damage will occur, and the longer it will take to heal. Stay in touch with the doctor at any stage of this healing/running process, follow his/her advice, and use your best judgement.

To allow for healing, once you have returned to exercise, stay below the threshold of further irritation. In other words, if the injury does not feel irritated at 2 miles, is a little irritated when running for 2.5 miles, and starts hurting a little at 3 miles, you should run no more than 2 miles. And if a runner's "healthy" run-walk ratio is 3 min run/1 min walk, when injured the ratio should be reduced to 1-1 or 30 seconds/30 seconds, or 30 seconds run/60 seconds walk.

When there is irritation of a "weak link" always allow a day of rest between exercise days. With most injuries you can cross-train to maintain conditioning, but make sure that your injury will allow this. Again, your doctor can advise.

Cross-training can maintain your conditioning

Before doing any of these, ask your doctor. Most are fine for most injuries, but some carry the risk of irritating the injured area and delaying the healing process. For more information on this, see the chapter on cross-training, in my GALLOWAY'S BOOK ON RUNNING SECOND EDITION or in this book. Gradually build up the cross-training, because you have to gradually condition muscles used in the new activity also. Very gentle walking is a great way to maintain conditioning if the injury and the doctor will allow it.

Treatment suggestions
—from one exerciser to another

Knee pain

Most knee problems will go away if you stop exercising immediately (don't run the the last mile when you think that you may have an injury) and take 5 days off. Ask your doctor if you can use anti-inflammatory medication. Try to figure out what caused the knee problem. Make sure that your run courses don't have a slant or canter. Look at the most worn pair of shoes you have, even street shoes. If there is wear on the inside of the forefoot, you probably overpronate. If you have repeat issues with knee pain, you may need a foot support or orthotic. If there is pain under the kneecap, or arthritis, the glucosamine/chondroitin products have helped. The best I've found in this category is Joint Maintenance Product by Cooper Complete.

Outside of the knee pain—Ilio-tibial band syndrome

This band of fascia acts as a tendon, running down the outside of the leg from the hip to just below the knee. The pain is most commonly noticed on the outside of the knee, but can occur anywhere along the band. I believe this to be a "wobble injury". When the muscles get tired, they don't keep you on a straight track. The I-T band tries to restrain the wobbling motion, but it cannot. By continuing to run, your wobbling motion will overuse the band. Most of the feedback I receive from exercisers and doctors is that once the healing has started (usually a few days off from exercise), most will heal as fast by gentle running and walking as they would from no running at all. In this case, however, it is crucial to get your doctor's OK to exercise, and then, to stay below the threshold of further irritation.

Treatment for Ilio-tibial band

1. Stretching: Stretching the I-T band releases the tightness that produces the pain. With this injury only, you can stretch before, after, and even during a workout. The primarily role for stretching is to allow you to keep going by releasing the tightness.

2. Self-massage using a foam roller. This device has helped thousands of exercisers get over this injury faster than any other treatment. On my website www.RunInjuryFree.com is a picture of someone using a foam roller. Put the roller on the floor, lie on it using body weight to press, and roll the area that is sore. Rolling before a run will help it "warm up", and rolling afterward often helps the injury recover faster. I also recommend rolling it at night.

3. Massage Therapy: a good massage therapist can tell whether massage will help, and where to massage. The two areas for possible attention are the connecting points of the connective tissue that is tight, and the fascia band itself, in several places. "The Stick" is a self-massage roller device that has also helped many exercisers recover from I-T band injuries while continuing to run. As with the foam roller, it helps to warm up the area before exercising, and to roll it out afterward.

4. Walking at a slow pace and with a gentle stride is usually fine—and usually you can find a run/walk/shuffle ratio that works. Again, maintain a short stride.

5. Direct ice massage on the area of pain: 15 minutes of continuous rubbing every night.

Shin pain—"shin splints" or stress fracture

Almost always, pain in this area indicates a minor irritation called "shin splint" that allows for gentle running as you heal. The greatest pain

or irritation during injury is at the beginning of a run, which gradually lessens or goes away during the workout. It takes several weeks (minimum) to fully heal, so you must have patience. Stay below the threshold of irritation!

- Inside pain—posterior shin splints. Irritation of the inside of the leg, coming up from the ankle is called "posterior tibial shin splints" and is often due to over pronation of the foot (foot rolls in at push-off).
- Front of shin—anterior shin splints. When the pain is in the muscle on the front of the lower leg it is "anterior tibial shin splints". This is very often due to having too long a stride when running and especially when walking. Downhill terrain should be avoided as much as possible during the healing process.
- Stress fracture. If the pain is in a very specific place, and increases as you run, you could have a more serious problem: a stress fracture. This is becoming increasingly more common in women who do speed training or race-walking technique, who exercise more than 3 days a week, who don't use enough walk breaks, and who keep increasing weekly mileage without strategic rest weeks. Stress fractures can indicate low bone density and calcium deficiency. If you even suspect a stress fracture, do not run or do anything stressful on the leg and see a doctor. Stress fractures take weeks of no exercise, and usually require wearing a cast for the first few weeks. It is crucial to be gentle during the first few weeks of healing. Those who have had stress fractures have a much higher tendency to get them again. Runners who've had them should walk a lot more often during all runs, and run no more often than every other day.

Heel pain—Plantar fascia

The most effective treatment is putting your foot in a supportive shoe before you step out of your bed in the morning. This very common injury (pain on the inside or center of the heel) is felt during the first steps after rising. As you get warmed up, the pain tends to gradually go away, only to return the next morning. Be sure to get a "shoe check" at a technical running store to make sure that you have the right shoe for your foot. If the pain is felt during the day, and is significant, you should consult with a podiatrist. Usually the doctor will construct a foot support that will surround your arch and heel. This does not always need to be a hard orthotic. Usually a softer one, designed for your foot, works quite well.

The "toe squincher" exercise can help develop foot strength that will also support the foot (done 15-30 times a day on both feet). This is simply done by pointing your toes and flexing the muscles in your foot for several seconds until you feel cramping.

Behind heel/Back of the foot—Achilles tendon

The Achilles tendon is the narrow band of tendon rising up from the heel and connecting to the calf muscle. It is part of a very efficient mechanical system, which works like a strong rubber band. The resulting action will leverage a lot of spring out of the foot, with a little effort from the calf muscle. It is usually injured due to excessive stretching, either through exercising or by stretching exercises. First, avoid any activity that stretches the tendon in any way. It helps to add a small heel lift to all shoes, which reduces the range of motion. Every night, rub a chunk of ice directly on the tendon. Keep rubbing for about 15 minutes, until the tendon gets numb. Bags of ice or frozen gels don't do any good at all, in my opinion. Usually after 3-5 days off from exercise, the icing takes hold and the Achilles feels stronger each day. Anti-inflammatory medication very rarely helps with the Achilles tendon, in my experience.

Gout—Toe joint pain (ankle, foot tenderness) with swelling

The swelling of the big toe joint, with pain, is commonly the result of an accumulation of uric acid in your foot. The pain may also be felt in the ankle, with significant and often debilitating tenderness on the bottom of the forefoot. Major causes are dehydration, alcohol consumption, and eating too much protein (particularly red meat). There are some effective drugs that can manage this problem. Drinking about 8 glasses of water a day, spaced throughout the day, is a good way to stay hydrated.

Hip and groin pain or tighteness

After a run/walk that is long for the individual, it is common for women to experience hip tightness and aches/pains. Women have wider hips that may have been "adjusted" during childbirth. Here are some common corrections.

Shorten stride—many women run and walk with a stride that is too long, causing the hips to rotate out of their natural range of motion.
Upright posture—hip aggravation is increased when the hips are shifted back (often called "sitting in the bucket". Imagine that you are a puppet on a string as you come out of each walk break.
More frequent walk breaks—from the beginning of your run, if you increase the frequency of your rest breaks for the muscles and tendons, you can significantly reduce the hip fatigue.

On extremely long runs, for the individual, there are often some "weak links" that get aggravated. Usually a normal dose of an anti-inflammatory medication can settle it down, after exercise. Check with your doctor to determine if this is appropriate for you.

Generally, stretching will aggravate the hips further, and should be avoided.

Calf muscle

The calf is the most important muscle for running. It is often irritated by stretching, running too fast when tired, by too many speed sessions without adequate rest between, and sprinting at the end of races or workouts.

Deep tissue massage has been the best treatment for most calf muscle problems experienced by my athletes and myself. Try to find a very experienced massage therapist who has helped lots of runners with calf problems. This can be painful but is about the only way to remove some bio-damage in the muscle. The "stick" can be very beneficial for working damage out of the calf muscle—on a daily basis (see www.JeffGalloway.com for more information on this product).

Don't stretch! Stretching will tear the muscle fibers that are trying to heal. Avoid running hills, and take very frequent walk breaks as you return to running.

31

Mental Toughness

- Consistency is the most important part of conditioning and fitness

- Motivation is the most important factor in being consistent

- You can gain control over your motivation—every day

The choice is yours. You can take control over your attitude, or you can let yourself be swayed by outside factors that will leave you on a motivational roller coaster: fired up one day, and down the next. Getting motivated on a given day can sometimes be as simple as saying a few key words and taking a run. But staying motivated requires a strategy or a motivational training program. To understand the process, we must first look inside your head.

The brain has two hemispheres that are separated and don't interconnect. The logical left brain does our business activities, trying to steer us into pleasure and away from discomfort. The creative and intuitive right side is an unlimited source of solutions to problems and connects us to hidden strengths.

As we accumulate stress, the left brain sends us a stream of logical messages that tell us "you don't need to exercise today", "you've got so much to do" "this isn't your day" and even philosophical messages like "why are you doing this." We are all capable of staying on track and maintaining motivation even when the left brain is saying these things. So the first step in taking command over motivation is to ignore the left brain unless there is a legitimate reason of health or safety (very rare). You can deal with the left brain, through a mental training program.

The following drills allow the right side of the brain to work on solutions to the problems you are having. As the negative messages spew out of the left brain, the right brain doesn't argue—it just goes to work, solving problems. By preparing mentally for the challenges you expect, you will empower the right brain to deal with the problems and to develop mental toughness. But even more important, you will gain confidence from just having a strategy comprised of proven ways to deal with the problems.

Rehearsing success

Getting out the door after a hard day

By rehearsing yourself through a motivation problem, you can be more consistent and set yourself up for improvement. You must first have a goal that is do-able, and a rehearsal situation that is realistic. Let's learn by doing:

1 State your desired outcome: To be walking/running from my house after a hard day

2. Detail the challenge: Low blood sugar and fatigue, a stream of negative messages, need to get the evening meal ready to be cooked, overwhelming desire to feel relaxed

3. Break up the challenge into a series of actions, which lead you through the mental barriers, no one of which is challenging to the left brain.

- You're driving home at the end of the day, knowing that it is a scheduled exercise day, but you have no energy
- Your left brain says: "You're too tired" "take the day off" "You don't have the energy to run"
- So you say to the left brain: "I'm not going to exercise. I'll put on some comfortable shoes and clothes, eat and drink, get food preparation going for dinner, and feel relaxed.
- You're in your room, putting on comfortable clothes and shoes (they just happen to be used for running)
- You're drinking coffee (tea, diet cola, etc) and eating a good tasting energy snack, as you get the food prepared to go into the oven
- Stepping outside, you check on the weather
- You're walking to the edge of your block to see what the neighbors are doing
- As you cross the street, you're on your way
- The endorphins are kicking in, you feel good, you want to continue

Lesson: a body on the couch wants to remain there. But once a body gets in motion, it wants to stay in motion.

4. Rehearse the situation over and over, fine-tuning it so that it becomes integrated into the challenges of your life and is in "synch" with the way you think and act.

5. Enjoy the reward. Finish by mentally focusing on the good feelings experienced with the desired outcome. You have felt the good attitude, the vitality, the glow from a good run, and you are

truly relaxed. So revisit these positive feelings at the end of each rehearsal.

Getting out the door early in the morning

The second most common motivational problem reported relates to the comfort of the bed, upon waking, when it's time for exercise.

State your desired outcome: To be walking/running away from the house early in the morning

Detail the challenge: Desire to lie in bed, no desire to exert yourself so early. The stress of the alarm clock, and having to think about what to do next when the brain isn't working very fast.

Break up the challenge into a series of actions, which lead you through the mental barriers, no one of which is challenging to the left brain.

- The night before, lay out your exercise clothes and shoes, near your coffee pot, so that you don't have to think.
- Set your alarm, and say to yourself over and over: alarm off, feet on the floor, to the coffee pot" or…."alarm, floor, coffee" As you repeat this, you visualize doing each action without thinking. By repeating it, you lull yourself to sleep. You have been programming yourself for taking action the next morning.
- The alarm goes off. You shut it off, put feet on the floor, and you head to the coffee pot—all without thinking.
- You're putting on one piece of clothing at a time, sipping coffee, without thinking about exercise.
- With coffee cup in hand, walk out the door to see what the weather is like.
- Sipping coffee, you walk to edge of your block or property to see what the neighbors are doing.
- Putting coffee down, you cross the street, and have made the break!
- The endorphins are kicking in, you feel good, you want to continue

Lesson: A body on the bed wants to stay on the bed. But once that body gets moving, it wants to keep moving.

Rehearsals lead to patterns of behavior more easily if you don't think—but just move from one action to the next. The power of the rehearsal is that you have formatted your brain for a series of continuous and connected actions. As you repeat the pattern, revising it for real life, you become what you want to be. You are successful!

Dirty tricks

The strategy of the rehearsal drill will get you focused, organized, out the door and down the road for a few miles. But on the really rough days, it helps to have some dirty tricks to play on the left side of the brain.

These "quick fixes" distract the left brain for a while, allowing you to move down the road for half a mile or so. Some call these images "imaginative" and others call them "crazy". They don't have to have any logic behind them. But when you counter a left-brain message with a creative idea you open a window of opportunity to get down the road.

The giant invisible rubber band

When I get tired on long or hard exercise sessions, I unpack this secret weapon, and throw it around someone ahead of me. For a while, the person doesn't realize that he or she has been "looped" and continues to push onward while I get the benefit of being pulled along. After a short period of getting into this image, I have to laugh at myself for believing in such an absurd notion—but laughing activates the creative right side of the brain. This usually generates several more entertaining ideas, especially when you do this on a regular basis. If you are exercising alone, wrap your rubber band around a pole or the rail of your treadmill.

The right brain has millions of dirty tricks. Once you get it activated, you are likely to experience solutions to problems you are currently having. It can entertain you as you get another 400-800 yards closer to your finish.

For many more dirty tricks and mental strategies, see *Galloway's Book on Running Second Edition* and *Marathon—You Can Do It*.

#32

The Clothing Thermometer

After years of coaching exercisers in various climates, here are my recommendations for the appropriate clothing based upon the temperature. The first layer, since it will be next to your skin, should feel comfortable, with technical fibers to move the moisture away from your skin. You may have to resist the temptation to buy a fashion color, but function is most important. Actually, more and more technical garments are attractively presented. As you try on the clothing in the store, watch for seams and extra material in areas where you will have body parts rubbing together, thousands of times during a run/walk (armpit, between legs).

Cotton is not a good fabric for those who perspire a great deal, as it absorbs the sweat, holding it next to your skin, and increasing the weight you must carry during the run. Garments made out of fabric labeled Polypro, Coolmax, Drifit, etc., can retain enough body heat to keep you warm in winter, while releasing the extra amount. By moving moisture to the outside of the garment, these technical fabrics help you stay cooler in summer, while avoiding the winter chill.

Temperature	What to wear
60°F and above (14°C +)	Tank top or singlet, and shorts
9°C to 13°C or 50 to 59°F	T-shirt and shorts
5 to 8°C or 40 to 49°F	Long sleeve light weight shirt, shorts or tights (or nylon long pants) Mittens and gloves
0 to 4°C or 30 to 39°F	Long sleeve medium-weight shirt, and another T-shirt, tights and shorts, Socks or mittens or gloves and a hat over the ears
-4 to −1°C or 20-29F	Medium-weight, long sleeve shirt, another T-shirt, tights and shorts, socks, mittens or gloves, and a hat over the ears
-8 to −3°C or 10-19°F	Medium-weight, long sleeve shirt, and medium/heavy-weight shirt, Tights and shorts, nylon wind suit, top and pants, socks, thick mittens And a hat over the ears
-12 to −7°C or 0-9°F	Two medium or heavy-weight long sleeve tops, thick tights, thick Underwear (especially for men), medium to heavy warm up, gloves and thick mittens, ski mask, a hat over the ears, and Vaseline covering any exposed skin.
-18 to −11°C or −15°F	Two heavyweight long sleeve tops, tights and thick tights, thick underwear (and supporter for men),

	thick warm up (top and pants), mittens over gloves, thick ski mask and a hat over ears, Vaseline covering any exposed skin, thicker socks on your feet and other foot protection, as needed.
Minus 20 both C & F	Add layers as needed

Fabulously Full Figured?

While we were writing this book, a growing number of women who are larger than the average citizen, asked for a chapter dealing with some special issues. After consulting with a variety of those who have fought these battles, and are still doing so successfully, the following information is offered with information on bras, diets, group support, etc.

85 pounds and counting

Tracy B added the usual weight during her pregnancy, and kept on going. When the scales told her that she was almost 100 pounds over her "healthy" weight, she walked out the door and kept going. A local charity marathon team provided her with a cause and good friends, as she walked her way to the marathon. "The marathon team I became a part of is like a little extension of my family." Instead of trying a restrictive diet, she simply tried reasonably sized meals and no high-fat snacks. She's still 10 pounds from her goal, but is still losing.

"Don't look at the big number of pounds you need to lose. Set an attainable goal, maybe 10 pounds at a time. And if you fall off the wagon, get back on and don't beat yourself up about it. Be proud of how hard you are working."

Tips from Tracy

1. "Never give up on yourself and be very proud of yourself for any effort you're making to make yourself healthier and fit.
2. Don't beat yourself up for "falling off the wagon" - this will happen at some point. Just dust yourself off and make that day your "first day" again - don't look back!
3. Don't let friends or family discourage your efforts. I know this sounds odd because these people should be your support system - but some people don't adapt to change very well and can feel threatened by the new you and your new group of friends.
4. Eat a very healthy, well-balanced diet. If you're not sure how to get started with this either consult this, book or check with your doctor or nutritionist.
5. Then make yourself a fat-burning machine. When I first started walking I would walk on my breaks at work, my lunch hour and then do my regular distance when I got home.
6. Be sure to cross-train. Not only is this good for your muscles, but it's good for your brain too.
7. You deserve your time to exercise!
   I think the biggest thing for women (no matter what size) to keep in mind is that you deserve to give this to yourself. My job and my family get me for 14 out of the 16 hours I put in a day. I allow myself to take those other 2 hours for me - guilt free! I need this - distance walking defines who I am. In return, my family gets a healthier and happier Mom! I want to be around to see my kids grow up and then run circles around my grandkids!"

Sherry's tips—more than 150 pounds lost...runs marathons

Exercise was the theme in rising out of depression and into a vigorous life. Be sure to read her moving and inspirational story later in this chapter Here are her key suggestions.

- "If you are considerably overweight/obese, see your doctor, and get good shoes from a good running store.
- Winded when doing even gentle exercise? Then walk slowly at first.

- Excess skin—use girdles, Spandex, knee-to-chest Flexee, that keeps it from getting in the way.
- Back issues: physical therapy can help. Ab strengthening helped a bit. The only thing that ultimately helped me was getting my excess skin removed after weight loss. Don't lean over or look down—stay upright!
- Make sure to shower and dry off properly. Excess skin and moisture is a prime habitat for a yeast infection.
- Larger women feel self-conscious when running/exercising. Ladies-only full-service gyms are a good supportive environment to get started. I found that my fellow runners are really nice people-no matter how much faster they are than you. As heavy as I was, I always got friendly waves and greetings on the running trails. Be proud, don't look down!
- Don't be afraid of your first race. Most races have a big walking group. Sign up with friends"....*Sherry*

Bras

Be prepared to pay significantly more than you would pay for your everyday bra—sometimes as much as you would pay for your shoes. Remember that bras usually last a lot longer than shoes.

There are a growing number of bras designed for specific types of exercise, based upon cup size. Many large-breasted women have reported success with the Enell brand and the Fiona model from Moving Comfort. Champion has a seamless underbra with underwire that has also been successful.

- Many of the well-constructed "workout bras" are not supportive for runners. The elastic in these products (for twisting and extraneous motion in tennis, Pilates, etc.) allows for significant bouncing and stress when running.

- Comfort: Look first at the fibers next to your skin. The micro fibers can move moisture away from your skin, reducing chafing (see next section), moisture chill, and weight increase due to the absorption of sweat by cotton and similar fibers.

C, D & E Cups: More support is needed. Look for a bra that will fit each breast, and a strap that has minimal or no elastic. The best placement of the straps will differ among individuals—so try on a variety of bras to find the configuration that matches up with your body. If you receive pressure on the shoulders, where the straps press down, padded straps can help. See the "Woman's Issues" chapter of this book for more on bra fitting.

Exercise improves health and well-being—even when obese. This is the finding of numerous studies at the Cooper Research Institute (Dallas, Texas) and other institutions. At Cooper, the obese-but-fit subjects were shown to have a healthier profile than sedentary, thin subjects.

Worried about the way they look in public, many heavier women don't exercise. That's too bad because it is clear that even 10 minutes of regular movement of the feet will bestow a better attitude, and can lead to higher self-esteem. Short exercise segments will also burn fat! It is easier to piece together several segments of 100-200 steps than 30 minutes at one time. Smaller segments tend to reduce appetite increase in most of the runners that we've heard from on the issue.

Read the fat-burning section of this book. The "set point" mechanism can help you understand fat deposition, and what you can do to hold your own—or lower it. And please, don't go on a restrictive diet. These usually produce water loss, and increased fat stores after the diet.

The low-carbohydrate scam

There is no doubt that low-carb diets can help you lose weight....water weight. Such a loss is superficial and easily gained back. Here's how it works. To perform physical exertion, you need a quick energy source called glycogen, which is a form of processed carbohydrate, that is stored in the muscles, liver and other areas. It must be replenished every day. The storage areas for glycogen are limited and glycogen is also the primary source for vital organs like the brain. A good quantity of water (needed in the use of glycogen) is stored near the glycogen storage areas.

By starving themselves of carbohydrates, low-carb dieters experience a severe reduction in glycogen. But if the glycogen isn't there, water is not stored either. The elimination of these two substances can produce a significant weight loss within days—continuing for a few weeks.

Fat is not being burned off. In fact, fat is often a significant ingredient in many of the low-carb diets. As low-carb dieters eat more fat, they often increase the fat on the body. But they don't realize this because the scales are showing a total loss—due to the water/glycogen reduction. When they replace water and glycogen later, the weight goes back on. Soon the overall body weight is greater than before because of the added fat from the low-carb diet.

Because the glycogen energy source is low or depleted, low-carbers will not have much energy for exercise. This is why you will hear folks on this diet complain of low energy, lack of desire to exercise, inability to finish a workout, and sometimes lack of mental focus (low glycogen means less fuel for the brain).

Even if you "tough it out" or cheat on the diet a little, your capacity to do even moderately strenuous exertions will be greatly reduced. With your energy stores near empty, exercising becomes a real struggle, and no fun. The reduction in exercise and movement in general usually results in a lower metabolism rate—meaning that you won't be burning many calories as you go about your life activities.

LOW CARB DIETS DON'T TELL YOU THIS.....

* You don't burn fat—many gain fat
* The weight loss is usually water loss, with glycogen loss
* Almost everyone on this diet resumes regular eating within a few weeks or months

- Almost all low-carb dieters gain back more weight than they lost
- You lose the energy and motivation to exercise
- You lose exercise capacity that can help to keep the weight off when you resume eating normally
- Your metabolism rate goes down—making it harder to keep the weight off

Group support is huge—join or start a charity fund raising or run-walk group, such as that for www.BreastCancerMarathon.com The programs at Weight Watchers and Curves can be very successful with group support.

98 pounds off...and still losing

Karen had been overweight most of her life, and, as she puts it, "definitely not athletic." But she had taken the path used by women through the ages: "I had tried every diet, spent an embarrassing amount of money on diet programs." The weight would drop for a few weeks or months and then, steadily rise until it surpassed the pre-diet amount. For some reason, surpassing 200, 225 and 250 pounds was OK. When the nurse told her she weighed 271, she held it in until reaching her car and then the tears flowed.

When her friend Jo decided to train for the Country Music Half-Marathon (Nashville), Karen was determined to use this race as a goal to be an every-other-day walker. Her fitness improved week by week, as she found the challenge of this 13-miler highly motivating. The run-walk-run method allowed her to move from a walker to a runner. So, in her late 30's, weighing 230 pounds Karen ran a minute and walked a minute. Sedentary spouse Paul was so impressed by her steady progress that he began running also, at 278 pounds. About 15 months later, Paul had lost 58 pounds. Karen has lost 98 pounds, and is still losing. As Karen approached the finish line of the Country Music 13.1 miler, the tears started flowing again—for all of the right reasons. Karen and Paul schedule vacations around running events now, and are on track for a big trip to the Chicago Marathon.

"If you're a beginner, start with short run - walk intervals. It's better to set realistic goals that you can meet and then adjust them as you improve." *Karen*

Sherry began her journey at 348 pounds

A normal 25-year-old female should be happy, healthy and full of life. At 25, I was lazy, super obese, unhealthy, depressed, and had minimal self-confidence. I always had a weight problem: 40 pounds overweight at 15, 70 pounds at 18. By the time I graduated college and married at age 22, I was an incredible 125 pounds overweight, and at my twenty-fifth birthday, I weighed 348 pounds!

"I cannot pinpoint one reason that led me to being super-obese with a BMI of 56. I did not have an easy time growing up. My older sister was gravely ill when I was young, and my mom had a difficult time dealing with depression and anxiety. At times I felt like I was not loved, which led to sexual abuse as a teenager. I was diagnosed with Polycystic Ovarian Syndrome (PCOS), which results in fertility problems and heightened levels of insulin resistance. I loved to eat carbs, which really packed on the pounds. It was an atrocious cycle-the more I would eat, the less I could exercise. The heavier I got, the more I became depressed, which led me to eating more to comfort myself."

"*My breaking point* My husband and I tried to start a family for months, with no success. Hormone therapy didn't work either and triggered hair loss in clumps, mood swings and hot flashes. I was miserable. Finally, we were scheduled to see a reproductive endocrinologist, but rejected because I was too heavy, and the pregnancy risks to me and the baby would be too great. I knew that I was on track for a heart attack, and I loved my husband too much to leave him tragically at a young age."

"*My decision* to change my life started with a gastric bypass operation. I lost weight quickly and easily because my stomach was now the size of an egg. My new stomach was a tool, and being successful at weight loss would be a life-long commitment. As soon as I was released from the hospital I began an exercise regimen, mall walking and a ladies-only gym. The exercise was helping to keep the fat off. Then, my friend Susan won an entry in the Peachtree Road Race, the world's largest 10k. I thought anyone who could run a 5k was an elite athlete! I was in awe when she finished the race in 80 minutes. Then came the great visualization: If she could do it, then so can I!

"Ready, set, go! There was no starting gun to signal the start of my training, but I sure was fired up. I set a goal of running in the Kaiser Permanente Corporate 5k, just over a month away. The night before the race I woke up in horrible pain at 2AM. My husband rushed me to the ER where they discovered I had a hole somewhere in my digestive system. I had emergency surgery, which led to a 14-inch scar, 40 staples, and a week's vacation at Gwinnett Medical Center. I was distraught. I felt that everything I worked hard to achieve was ruined. I cried for three hours straight. The nurses tried to make me feel better, but I was inconsolable. At this point, my only dream was shattered."

"A week after being released from the hospital, I started walking, even with pain. I signed up for a local 10K, trained and finished—I was a runner! I immediately found my husband and announced I wanted to run a marathon. He pretty much thought I was insane, but I joined a training group, dealt with the gastric/fluid absorption problems, excessive loose skin and back pain. I crossed the Chicago Marathon finish line and a wave of emotions overcame me. At 348 pounds, I never once imagined being able to run to my mailbox. Through many trials and tribulations, and mostly hard work, I was able to lose the weight and do what I once thought was unthinkable."

"Through sweat, hard work, and even a few tears, I was able to accomplish each of the goals I set for myself because I developed a strong mental attitude, and took charge over my health and fitness. I had the seeds of these capabilities when I was a depressed 348-pounder—and didn't know it. You do too. Ironman Florida – here I come!"

Major Differences as You Get Older

As mentioned above, research shows that runners tend to experience fewer orthopedic problems as they age than those who don't exercise regularly. But we have known runners who've ignored common sense, pushed through repeated warning signs, and encountered self-imposed permanent damage. It is clear to us that if you walk and/or run regularly, below the threshold of irritation, your joints continue to adapt and maintain their functions better over a longer period of time.

Mature exercisers often compare themselves to old cars. Due to continued wear and tear, there are aches and pains that will be experienced. If you make the right conservative training adaptations, most can reduce the flareups, and keep going when the "weak links" complain. In dealing with the problems, you get to know yourself better, and can take action to prevent problems. Most of the adjustments involve adding strategic rest, such as exercising every other day, taking more walk/shuffle breaks, inserting extra recovery time when aches and pains increase, and having a doctor as a health coach who wants to keep you exercising.

Competitive runners will notice a natural slowdown in their pace and race performance as they age. The slowdown increases after the age of 60-65. With some smart adjustments, this slowdown can be reduced. Mature competitive runners must continually ask themselves a difficult question, every few months: How much risk do I want to take by running faster? Those who continue to push the limits usually reduce the number of years that they can enjoy running at any speed. This is where real maturity counts: make a choice and take the consequences. It is my recommendation that the enjoyment of exercise be the primary goal. There's a lot more information on age-related issues in Jeff's book RUNNING UNTIL YOU'RE 100.

How to deal with the recovery rate slowdown

After the age of 30, it takes longer for the legs to feel fresh and bouncy after a strenuous run. Most runners don't notice this (or don't want to admit it) until they reach the age of 40. By adding conservative training ingredients, injury risk drops dramatically. Many veterans find that they run faster while covering fewer miles per week—especially when running fewer days per week.

The best way we've found to speed recovery is to include strategic rest days before and after strenuous exercise days. This allows the body to rebuild and adapt to efficient running. In general, it is better to cover more miles on certain key days and then avoid the use of the same muscles, the next day (cross training is fine). The following table has recommendations for the number of days one can run, based upon age, for runners who:

- Are experiencing more injuries, aches and pains, or orthopedic problems
- Are not recovering quickly between the more difficult sessions
- Are experiencing a slowdown in race times

(If you're not having any of these problems you can run the number of days per week that you wish)

Recommended number of running/walking days per week by age:

(You can walk or cross train on 2-3 other days if desired)

35 and under: no more than 5 days a week
36-45: no more than 4 days a week
46-59: every other day
60 + : 3 days a week
70 + : 2 longer run days and 1 walk day
80 + : One longer run/walk, one shorter run/walk, and one very easy short walk

Note: The day before the long run should be a day of rest.

More walk breaks

The simple addition of more walk breaks from the beginning of exercise has allowed many mature runners to maintain mileage while reducing aches and pains.

Adjustments for Runners Pace per mile	Run Amount	-	Walk Amount
7:00	4 minutes		20 seconds
7:30	4 minutes		25 seconds
8:00	4 minutes		30 seconds
8:30	3 minutes		30 seconds
9:00	2 minutes		30 seconds
9:30	2 minutes		40 seconds
10:00-11:30	1:30		30 seconds
11:30-13:30	1 minute		30 seconds
13:30-14:59	30 seconds		30 seconds (or 1-1)
15:00-17:00	30 seconds		45 seconds
17:00-20:00	20-30 seconds		1 minute

A longer and easier warm-up

As the years go by, it takes longer (during an individual run or walk) for the legs to feel good. Here is what I recommend:

- At least 5 minutes of very gentle walking
- Then 5 minutes of walking at varied paces. Even if you walk a bit faster during the second 5 minutes, use a short stride.
- Runners will then insert some run breaks into your walk for 10 minutes. Start with 10-20 seconds of running followed by a minute of walking, then gradually shift to a minute of running and a minute of walking—or 30 sec/30 sec.
- Runners should then ease into your running pace, and follow the run-walk-run frequency for that day.
- It is always better to be conservative—walk or shuffle more frequently if needed.

Breaking up your daily mileage into 2 or 3 sessions

A runner recently told Jeff that her fitness improved during the year after she retired from her career in nursing. Instead of walking her 3 miles once a day, she walked 2 miles in the morning and 2-3 miles in the afternoon. She enjoyed the vitality boost from both sessions.

Fast running takes more out the legs

Runners in their 40s and 50s can sometimes do the same workouts they ran in their 20s and 30s—but they will pay dearly for this. Running at your limits after a certain age takes an increasingly longer recovery time. While it is true that speed training and racing significantly increase the chance of injury, there are safer ways to train to improve times at any age. It's a fact that as you age, recovery elements must be added to the program. I don't recommend speed reps after 80 years of age, but there is some speed benefit from my Cadence Drills and Acceleration Gliders, mentioned in this book.

Fine-tuning from previous years

As much as we would like to improve memory, this will probably not happen. Making good notes in your journal will allow you to analyze the causes of aches and pains, and training problems. Even if you can't run faster at age 90, you can run smarter, and prevent problems. Use the margins of your journal. Tell yourself what you want to do the next time to avoid problems. You'll help yourself greatly by tracking the adjustments. As you embark on another goal in future years, you'll have a better blueprint, because you've improved the original plan through adjustments to your reality.

We believe that a great deal of the satisfaction we receive emerges from what we do on a regular basis. We've seen many people improve their outlook on life itself when they use a proven plan to improve their fitness. Following and adjusting your plan is almost always a life-changing experience, for the better.

Blood sugar issues

Many exercisers develop blood sugar problems as they age. Read the chapter in this book on blood sugar maintenance.

Health issues

Running and walking make you feel better as they enhance health potential and life expectancy. Many runners have told me that their running gave them the only signs of serious health risks—which led to early detection and successful treatment. Find a doctor who supports running and wants to work with you to sustain the highest level of wellness.

Iris: Running like 80!

Iris began her running career at the young age of 54. She was overweight, had high blood pressure and high cholesterol, and was depressed. After only a few months she decided to attempt a local 10-mile race and became convinced that she would die. She even told her sons where to find her will and bank vault key, and special instructions: "DO RESUSCITATE!"

After struggling through this very tough first race, and finishing, Iris became convinced that she could do almost anything. At the age of 54 she enrolled as a freshman at North Carolina State University and graduated with honors in just over 3 years. She has become what she always wanted to be: a professional writer.

She began her marathon career at age 74 and is just getting warmed up.

Products that Enhance Running

The following products will help all runners. For more information on these, visit www.JeffGalloway.com.

Other Galloway Books

Training schedules, and gifts that keep on giving—even to yourself. (Order them autographed from www.JeffGalloway.com)

Walking: Walkers now have a book that explains the many benefits, and how to maximize them, with training programs for 5K, 10K, Half- and Full-Marathons. There is resource information on fat-burning, nutrition, motivation and much more.

Getting Started: This is more than a state-of-the-art book for beginners. It gently takes walkers into running, with a 6-month schedule that has been very successful. Also included is information on fat-burning, nutrition, motivation, and body management. This is a great gift for your friends or relatives who can be "infected" positively by running.

A Year-Round Plan: You'll find daily workouts for 52 weeks, for three levels of runners: to finish, to maximize potential, and time improvement. It has the long runs, speed sessions, drills, hill sessions, all listed, in the order needed to do a 5K, 10K, Half- and Marathon during one year. Resource material is included to help with many running issues.

Galloway's Book On Running 2nd Edition: This is the best-seller among running books since 1984. Thoroughly revised and expanded in 2001, you'll find training programs for 5K, 10K, Half-Marathon, with nutrition, fat-burning, walk breaks, motivation, injuries, shoes, and much more. This is a total resource book

Marathon: This has the information you need to train for the classic event. There are training programs, with details on walk breaks, long runs, marathon nutrition, mental marathon toughness and much more.

Half-Marathon: This new book provides highly successful and detailed training schedules for various time goals, for this important running goal. Information is provided on nutrition, mental preparation, fluids, race day logistics & check list, and much more.

Testing Yourself: Training programs for 1 mile, 2 mile, 5K, and 1.5 mile are detailed, along with information on racing-specific information in nutrition, mental toughness, running form. There are also some very accurate prediction tests that allow you to tell what is a realistic goal. This book has been used effectively by those who are stuck in a performance rut at 10K or longer events. By training and racing faster, you can improve running efficiency and your tolerance for waste products, like lactic acid.

Running Until You're 100: In the chapter on joint health, you'll see in the research studies that runners have healthier joints than sedentary folks. In the chapter on the researched health benefits of exercise, an expert on longevity says that for every hour we exercise we can expect to get back 2 hours of life extension. Among those in the heroes section is an 85-year-old who recently finished his 700th marathon and will do 29 more this year. There are nutrition suggestions from Nancy Clark, training adjustments by decade, and many other helpful hints for running past the century mark.

Fit Kids—Smarter Kids: This book is a handbook for parents, teachers, youth leaders in how to lead kids into fitness that is fun. A growing number of studies are listed that document how kids who exercise do better in academics, and in life. Nancy Clark gives tips on what to eat, and there's a chapter on childhood obesity— with the hope that others, like the author (a former fat kid), can turn things around. There are resources, successful programs, inspirational stories and much more.

Running schools and retreats

Jeff conducts motivating running schools and retreats. These feature individualized information, form evaluation, comp- rehensively covering running, nutrition, and fat burning.

Podfitness—coaching through the iPod

As an extension of Jeff's training programs. He has teamed up with Podfitness.com to bring these workouts into your daily life. Now, you can have a custom program, during which Jeff coaches you through every training session on your iPod.

"My Podfitness training program is designed to reinforce what you've read here. Your program is designed expressly for you, and changes with you. You'll hear me throughout your workout, offering advice and encouragement. Plus, it lays your music in the background, which I think makes each run even more enjoyable." *JG*

Go to http://www.podfitness.com/jeffgalloway/ and they'll let you try it for free. I'm positive you'll be as impressed with it as I was, and that you'll become a better runner for it.

The stick

This massage tool can help the muscles recover quicker. It will often speed up the recovery of muscle injuries or iliotibial band injuries (on the outside of the upper leg, between knee and hip). This type of device can warm up the leg muscles and reduce the aggravation of sore muscles and tendons. By promoting blood flow during and after a massage, muscle recovery time is reduced.

To use "the stick" on the calf muscle (most important in running), start each stroke at the Achilles tendon and roll up the leg toward the knee. Gently roll back to the origin and continue, repeatedly. For the first 5 minutes a gentle rolling motion will bring additional blood flow to the area. As you gradually increase the pressure on the calf during an "up" stroke, you'll usually find some "knots" or sore places in the muscles. Concentrate on these as you roll over them again and again, gradually breaking up the tightness. See www.RunInjuryFree.com for more info on this.

Foam roller—self massage for I-T Band, Hip, etc.

This cylinder of dense foam is about 6" in diameter and about one foot long. We've not seen any mode of treatment for ilio-tibial band injury that has been more effective. For best effect, put the roller on the floor, and lie on your side so that the irritated I-T band area is on top of the roller. As your body weight presses down on the roller, roll up and down on the area of the leg you want to treat. Roll gently for 2-3 minutes and then apply more pressure as desired. This is actually a deep tissue massage that you can perform on yourself. For I-T band, we recommend rolling it before and after running. See www.RunInjuryFree.com for more info on this product.

Cryo-cup—best tool for ice massage

Rubbing with a chunk of ice on a sore area (when near the skin) is very powerful therapy. We know of hundreds of cases of Achilles tendon problems that have been healed by this method. The Cryo-Cup is a very convenient device for ice massage. The plastic cup has a plastic ring that sits on top of it. Fill it up with water, then freeze. When you have an ache or pain that is close to the skin, take the product out of the freezer, pour warm water over the outside of the cup to release it, and hold onto the plastic handle like an ice "popcicle". Rub constantly up and down the affected area for about 15 minutes, until the tendon (etc.) is numb. When finished, fill the cup and place in the freezer. In my experience, rubbing with a plastic bag of ice—or a frozen gel product—does no good at all in most cases.

YOU CAN DO IT—motivational audio CD

Put this in your car player as you drive to your run. You'll be motivated by the stories as you learn the strategies and methods that have allowed runners to deal with the negative messages of the left side of the brain—and push to their potential.

Endurox Excel

Many runners over 50 years old have told us that they have noticed a significantly faster muscle rebound when using this product. An hour before a long or hard workout, Jeff takes two of these Excel pills. Among the anti-oxidants is the active ingredient from gensing: ciwega. Research has shown that recovery time is reduced when this product is taken. We also use it when our legs have been more tired than usual for 2-3 days in a row.

Accelerade

This sports drink has a patented formula shown to improve recovery. Drinking it before and after prolonged, dehydrating workouts also helps to improve hydration. We recommend having a half-gallon container of Accelerade in the refrigerator. Drink 4-8 oz every 1-2 hours throughout the day. Best time to "top off" your fluid levels is within 24-hours before a long run. Prime time for replacing fluids is during the 24-hour period after a long run. Many runners have 32 oz or so in a thermos, for sipping during walk breaks in a prolonged speed-training session. I suggest adding about 25% more water than recommended.

Research has also shown that drinking Accelerade about 30 minutes before running can get the body's startup fuel (glycogen) activated more effectively, and may conserve the limited supply of this crucial fuel.

Endurox R4

This product has almost "cult following" status among runners. In fact, the research shows that the 4-1 ratio of carbohydrate to protein helps to reload the muscle glycogen more quickly (when consumed within 30 minutes of the finish of a hard or long workout. This means that the muscles feel bouncy and ready to do what you can do, sooner. There are other anti-oxidants in R4 that speed recovery.

Jeff Galloway's Training Journal

Some type of journal is recommended to organize, and track, your training plan. JEFF GALLOWAY'S TRAINING JOURNAL can be ordered from www.JeffGalloway.com, autographed. It simplifies the process, with places to fill in information for each day. There is also space for recording the unexpected thoughts and experiences that make so many runs come alive again as we read them.

Your journal allows you to take control over the organization of your training components. As you plan ahead and then compare notes afterward, you are empowered to learn from your experience, and make positive changes.

Galloway PC Coach—interactive software

This software will not only set up a marathon training program, it will help you to stay on track. As you log in, you're told if your training is not what it should be for that day. Sort through various training components quickly, and often find reasons why you are tired or have more aches and pains, etc.

Vitamins

I now believe that most runners need a good vitamin to boost the immune system and resist infection. There is some evidence that getting the proper vitamin mix can also speed recovery. The vitamin

ine I use is called Cooper Complete. Dr. Kenneth Cooper (founder of
the Cooper Clinic and the Aerobics Institute), is behind this product.
In the process of compiling the most formidable body of research on
exercise and long-term health I've seen anywhere, he found that
certain vitamins play important roles. www.coopercomplete.com

Buffered salt tablets—to reduce cramping

If your muscles cramp on long or hard runs, due to salt depletion,
this type of product may help greatly. The buffered sodium and
potassium tablets get into the system more quickly. Be sure to ask
your doctor if this product is OK for you (those with high blood
pressure, especially). If you are taking a statin drug for cholesterol,
and are cramping, it is doubtful that this will help. Ask your doctor
about adjusting the medication before long runs.

CONTROL OVER PACE BY GPS AND OTHER DISTANCE-PACE CALCULATORS

There are two types of devices for measuring distance, and both
are usually very accurate: GPS and accelerometer technology.
While some devices are more accurate than others, most will tell
you, almost exactly how far you have run/walked. These will allow
you to gain control over your pace—from the first 10th of a mile.

Freedom! With these devices, you can run/walk your long ones
wherever you wish, instead of having to repeat a loop—just
because it is measured. Instead of going to a track to do a "magic
mile", you can very quickly measure your segments on roads, trails
or residential streets.

The GPS devices track your movements by the use of navigational
satellites. In general, the more satellites, the more accurate the
measurement. There are "shadows" where the signals cannot be
acquired: buildings, forest, or mountains. On trails with lots of
small turns, the device may cut the tangents as it accounts for the
mileage. These are usually temporary interruptions, but will tend to
give a mileage reading than is less than the distance you actually
ran/walked.

The accelerometer products require a very easy calibration and have been shown to be very accurate. The "chip" on your shoe, is very sensitive to movement and effort, and sends the data to the wrist monitor. I've not heard of any pattern of technical interference with this technology. I've found it best during the calibration, to use a variety of paces, taking a walk/shuffle break or two in order to simulate what you will be doing when you run/walk.

Some devices require batteries, and others can be re-charged. Experienced staff members at a technical running store can often advise you on the pros and cons of each product. Sometimes they'll also share the "gossip" on the various brands and models, gained from the feedback they receive from customers.

Advisors:

John Cantwell, MD
Nancy Clark, RD,
Terry Davis, MD
Julie Gazmararian, MPH, PhD
Nicole Hagedorn, DO, OB/GYN
Dave Hannaford, DPM
Ruth Parker, MD
Diana Twiggs, MD
Wendy Welch, MD

Photo & Illustration Credits

Cover design: Sabine Groten
Cover photos: Imago, Mizuno
Inside photos: Mizuno, Norm Drews, getty images, Andy Sharp